CAPTAINS' LOGS

SUPPLEMENTAL II

By Mark A. Altman and Edward Gross

First published in the UK 1995 by
BOXTREE LTD
Broadwall House
London SE1 9PL

First published in the USA 1995 by
Image Publishing

10 9 8 7 6 5 4 3 2 1

This publication is not licensed by, nor is Boxtree or Image Publishing affiliated with, Paramount Pictures. This is a scholarly work, intended to explore the history of *Star Trek*.

No photos appearing in this book are copyright Paramount Pictures.

The illustrations on pages 17, 26, 40-42, 44, 50, 52-54, 57 are advertisements that were placed in TV Guide (USA) by New York's WPIX

ISBN: 0 7522 0938 8

Book design by Paul Nicosia
Jacket design by Peter Bridgewater

A catalogue record for this book is available from the British Library

Printed and bound in Great Britain by
Butler & Tanner Ltd, Frome and London

• • C O N T E N T S • •

Introduction 4

Season Seven: Journey's End 5

The Episodes 16

    "Descent, Part II" 17

    "Liaisons" 18

    "Interface" 21

    "Gambit, Parts I & II" 23

    "Phantasms" 25

    "Dark Page" 27

    "Attached" 28

    "Force of Nature" 30

    "Inheritance" 33

    "Parallels" 33

    "The Pegasus" 35

    "Homeward" 37

    "Sub Rosa" 38

    "Lower Decks" 39

    "Thine Own Self" 41

    "Masks" 42

    "Eye of the Beholder" 43

    "Genesis" 45

    "Journey's End" 46

    "Firstborn" 49

    "Bloodlines" 50

    "Emergence" 52

    "Preemptive Strike" 52

    "All Good Things" 54

Star Trek: Generations 63

Meeting The Press: Cast and Crew Interviews 72

Rick Berman (Producer) 72

David Carson (Director) 84

Patrick Stewart 92

Brent Spiner 100

Malcolm McDowell 109

William Shatner 116

Appendix A: The Final Trek 125

Appendix B: Saturday Night Stewart 127

Appendix C: Breast Of Both Worlds 128

• • • •

CAPTAINS' LOGS: SUPPLEMENTAL II
AN INTRODUCTION

They say that all good things must end, and it's that inevitability that greeted the seventh season of *Star Trek: The Next Generation*.

Seven years and 178 hours later, the starship Enterprise was finally put into dry dock. Its tenure there, however, was short-lived as witnessed by the 1995 British release of the motion picture *Star Trek: Generations*, which brings together Captains Jean Luc Picard (Patrick Stewart) and James T. Kirk (William Shatner). Given this fact, it seems almost difficult to mourn the show's passing, particularly when noting that there are *two* series on the air to replace it: *Star Trek: Deep Space Nine* and *Star Trek: Voyager*.

Somehow the ongoing *Star Trek* phenomenon is a bit difficult to fathom, particularly when looking back to 1986 at the time that *Next Generation* was first announced. Back then, there were very few people who believed that this new Enterprise would fly; that it would be impossible to replace Kirk, Spock, McCoy and the rest from the original series. Well, time has obviously proven otherwise. The original series is a rarity on television these days, yet every where you look there are stations showing at least one of its three spin-offs.

What you are holding is the third volume in a series designed to bring you behind the scenes of every voyage of the Enterprise in all its incarnations. Within these pages you'll find a complete episode guide to the seventh season of *Star Trek: The Next Generation*. Beyond that, we look at the making of *Generations* through personal interviews with producer Rick Berman, director David Carson and actors Patrick Stewart, Brent Spiner, Malcolm McDowell and William Shatner.

All good things must end? As usual, *Star Trek* refuses to play by the rules.

Edward Gross
Mark A. Altman

• • • •

SEASON SEVEN
Journey's End!

Nestled between photo credits from prestigious network shows and a cardboard standee of Captain Picard, there's a sign that hangs on the door of *Next Generation* executive producer Jeri Taylor's office that reads "Future Home of the Pygmy Marmosetts."

The cardboard sign, with its brightly stenciled lettering, seems somewhat out of place in Taylor's office and yet in some strange way it epitomizes the intangible *Trek* philosophy that Taylor has attempted to perpetuate on television during her tenure as one of the show's big three; sharing the producing reins with great birds Rick Berman and Michael Piller.

Says Taylor of the sign's origin, "A couple of freelance writers had come in and pitched a story which appealed to me because it was a very sweet, sensitive and emotional story which was a little hokey. Basically, it was about Beverly and Troi saving the last of an endangered species so that they could mate and procreate. When I called the staff down and told them about this story we were

going to develop, they began to snicker, and then laugh, and finally they began to guffaw.

"By the time I was done with this, everybody was on the floor howling and shrieking with laughter, all of them thinking I had absolutely lost my mind because of this story that I had found so appealing. And even as I said it, I began to have my doubts about it," she admits. "Yet, there was something very, nice at the core. We did try to develop the story and it proved very difficult to make work and it never went any place. But shortly after that, the staff went to Las Vegas for what they called a retreat to come up with story ideas. While they were there, in one of the big hotels, they happened upon a gallery which was soon to become a kind of petting zoo; and all along the walls were these placards, which said, 'Future Home of the Bunny Rabbit' and such. They saw one that said 'Future Home of the Pygmy Marmosetts' and decided that I must have it for my door, so they stole it from the hotel and scurried out into the night. When I came in on Monday morning, it was sitting on my door and there it remains."

The sign, which greets everyone who enters Taylor's office, reminds people that *Star Trek*'s formula, which has

proven the closest thing to alchemy for Paramount Pictures, is an uneasy mix of moralizing, allegory, personal challenges, science-fiction and a little bit of hokiness. It's an uneasy concoction and when it's ingredients are mixed right, *Star Trek* can be both intoxicating and inspiring. When done wrong, it can be downright insipid. *Star Trek: The Next Generation*'s seventh and final season episodes boasted their fair share of both qualities.

Star Trek's final year on the air presented the show's staff with some of its greatest challenges. It also proved one of the most difficult seasons for its writers, who were charged with creating another 26 hours of engaging television viewing while its producers continued to expand the franchise in new directions.

"I'm not sure how everything got done," says Taylor, who supervised the writing staff of producers Ronald D. Moore, Brannon Braga, executive story editor Rene Echevarria and story editor Naren Shankar, during its final season. "Rick Berman not only took on developing a new series, *Voyager*, but also continued the development of a feature film. I think we were all been kind of pushed to our limits and there were several things that made the season uniquely difficult."

• • • •

NO. 221 · MAY 6, 1994

Entertainment WEEKLY

'TREK'

INSIDE THE TENSE FINAL DAYS

THE 'NEXT GENERATION' CAST:
PATRICK STEWART, GATES McFADDEN,
BRENT SPINER, LEVAR BURTON,
JONATHAN FRAKES, MICHAEL DORN,
AND MARINA SIRTIS

Among the biggest challenges were that the show's senior writers, Moore and Braga, had been hired to write the first *Next Generation* feature film (*Generations*) precluding their full-time involvement early in the season. By the end of the year, Taylor herself was immersed in work on the spin-off series, *Voyager*, which she would co-create with Berman and Piller, who himself was attempting to streamline the second season of *Deep Space Nine*.

Says Rene Echevarria, "I did a lot of writing seventh season. I went from one teleplay to another. By the end of the season, I literally went from finishing an episode to doing a rewrite of another episode in five days to starting an episode that was due five days later. I wrote three episodes in the time you ordinarily have to write one. I was writing ten pages a day to get it done."

The stress of the season also took it's toll on the actors as evidenced by the rash of bad press they received during the weeks preceding the airing of the final episode. "The poor cast was exhausted," says Taylor. "Patrick who directed 'Preemptive Strike,' just before the finale was in every scene of this final episode and was really going on adrenaline. I think everybody was stretched

thin, but nobody slacked off."

Despite the myriad of complications, few would argue that the seventh season did boast several standout episodes. However, one wouldn't have forseen the quality of some of its later episodes based on the less than auspicious beginning of the season.

"I think that everybody pretty much would agree that the seventh season got off to a bit of a rocky start," offers Naren Shankar. "I think a lot of it had to do with the fact that we went out of the sixth season on a real roll and it was creatively very exhausting and, unfortunately, we never really got a break between seasons. Rene managed to get away for a couple of weeks but I had less than a week of vacation to get back. Ron and Brannon went to Hawaii and wrote the feature and came back immediately and we just jumped right in. As a result, I think the beginning of the season shows a little bit of exhaustion and it's unfortunate. You never sit down and say you want this season to suck."

Among the concerns of the staff seventh season was that a longtime prohibition against using the crutch of characters' relatives was frequently being broken. "I complained about that trend all year," says Brannon Braga who notes that such episodes

as "Interface," "Inheritance" and "Bloodlines" all involved relatives of the crew. "The one thing I was very disappointed about is that in almost every other show we were introducing a new family member. I found that to be embarrassing. I thought shows like 'Homeward' could have been done without a family member involved. It was somewhat arbitrary."

Echoes Shankar, "Ron Moore started calling it the season of lost souls. You don't set out at the beginning of the season to say we're going to do many relatives this season. It just happened. We even almost had Geordi's sister in 'Force Of Nature.' It's almost amusing in an embarrassing sort of way."

In fact, if it could be said that "Chain of Command" [the episode in which Picard is captured and tortured by the Cardassians] signaled a departure for the series sixth year in graduating from high concept storytelling — like the holodeck western "Fistful of Datas" and the transporter twilight zone of "Realm of Fear" — to compelling character drama, it was "Force of Nature," a show in which the crew discovers that warp drive is destroying the fabric of the universe, that had a profound effect on the writers during the seventh year — however, in a far less positive way.

"'Force of Nature' was something I fought for early on and went to the wall for," says Ron Moore. "We had a big meeting with Rick and Mike and Jeri and we all got on our high horses and we went in there and said we felt strongly about the episode saying, 'We want to do this, we want to make a statement, and we want to change the *Star Trek* universe forever. This is important and this is right and we should do it!' Now, I'm just going, 'What was I thinking?' because now we have this warp speed limit and in every third episode we have to get permission to go fast. It was such a great idea in concept. We always said that dealing with the environment on this show is incredibly difficult. It's hard to do a show about the ozone, because the ozone is huge and non-personal, and hard to make dramatic. We thought we had found a way to personalize it and make it our problem and it became `Force of Nature'."

Comments Michael Piller, "The truth is I spent so much time on *Deep Space Nine*, particularly at the beginning of the year, that my involvement with *The Next Generation* was that of a Monday morning quarterback. It made me feel uncomfortable

at times, sort of being an absentee landlord coming to collect the rent. I would come in to check the stories and read the scripts and give notes, but I felt seventh season my influence was beginning to lessen. It was almost two years since I had been in the room with the guys breaking stories, and these are very good people who deserved to be able to try the things that they always wanted to do."

However, Piller also realized early into the season that the show was not heading in a direction he was pleased with. "'Force Of Nature' certainly inspired us to have several long meetings on where the season was going," recalls Piller. "I felt we were letting it slip away."

As a result, Piller became adamant that the writers begin to re-dedicate themselves to the show and begin to address long-festering character issues. This ultimately led to show's like "Journey's End" in which Wesley chooses to leave Starfleet Academy, and "Bloodlines" in which Ferengi Daimon Bok returns to confront Picard.

"The problem was that we didn't have a lot of ideas," says Piller. "We had to go with the best ones we could come up with and then within each one of those execute it as best as we could. I was unhappy

with the first third of the season, but then I thought we really hit our stride. I was mostly inspired by the emotional impact on myself and others of the Beverly/Jean-Luc 'Attached' episode. That episode did not work in a couple of ways, but the way it did work was to fundamentally go to the heart of the series and force two characters that had a subtext of a relationship burning for some seasons, to finally confront those feelings. I found the emotional resonance so affecting and meaningful, that I said to Jeri let's spend what little time we have left really working on tying up some loose ends. I think that really inspired much of the last half of the season."

"Despite the people who say *Star Trek* is science-fiction and not a serious drama, we were able to actually get into some very deep human emotions. And that's one of the things I love about the show," says Nick Sagan, the freelance writer who pitched the show and receives screen credit for the teleplay. "I was pretty thrilled with the way 'Attached' turned out. I thought it was just gorgeously directed from beginning to end. The performances were fantastic. I ran into Gates McFadden and I thanked her and she thanked me. It was a real nice conversation. I told

Issue
#6
$5.95

Epi-log Journal

The Television Journal of Science Fiction, Fantasy, and Adventure

Jan.
-Feb.
1993

Gene Roddenberry Tribute Issue!

her she made me look really good and she said that I had helped turn the season around for her. She had been kind of down on *Trek* after doing it so long and my episode, and then 'Sub Rosa' and her directing, really turned everything around."

"There were about five episodes in the middle of seventh season that were as strong a group of episodes as I ever been a part of, going from 'Parallels' to 'Pegasus' to 'Lower Decks', which was really one of the wonderful shows of the year," says Michael Piller. "I also thought that the Beverly Crusher romance with the ghost ['Sub Rosa'] was a very well executed show. It was a terrific group of episodes. I thought we were doing as good as we possibly could. But the appetite of the season begins to gnaw at you and finally you have to say we have to do a show next week — what are we going to do?"

Jeri Taylor admits that each year it gets harder and harder to find things that haven't been dealt with before. "I talked to Patrick [Stewart] and Brent [Spiner] at one point and asked if there was any facet of their characters that they thought we hadn't explored yet, and both of them turned to me and said, 'Nope'," she smiles. "They couldn't come up with anything."

Piller admits that the fact that the writers stopped taking pitches — in which prospective writers try to sell ideas to the show — for several weeks during the season was a mistake and helped contribute to the dearth of workable story premises.

One result of the lack of story ideas coupled with Piller's newfound willingness to allow the writers to develop concepts which would have previously not been approved, were some pushing of the traditional *Trek* boundaries both in terms of interpersonal conflict and storytelling. Says Ron Moore, "I think the final year we thought the magic formula was just to break the rules, based on the success of the sixth season, and then we started hunting for something to do differently, like introducing warp drive limitations and stuff like that, but then started realizing, so what?"

Among the more radical ideas incorporated into the narrative tapestry of seventh season was the Worf / Troi romance which first blossoms in "Parallels," Brannon Braga's story of an alternate timeline in which the two officers are married.

"This was something we had been talking about for quite a while," says Taylor. "'Fistful of Datas,' for instance, was an effort to gradually bring

Worf and Troi a little closer together. Their romance just sort of erupted into bloom at the end of this season and I think has given us some very nice moments. It was unexpected and not what the fans predicted and I think that that's good. I've probably gotten more antagonistic mail on this than anything."

The emerging romance between Troi and Worf precluded the Troi/Riker relationship from moving to the forefront — although several of the writer's were anxious to provide that storyline with a sense of closure.

Offers Echevarria, "We were talking about how we wanted to marry Riker and Troi and we thought the fans would love that. Michael and Rick didn't care for that idea. Michael wanted to explore the Worf-Troi relationship. The actors were not happy about it. Marina has always maintained that Riker is her Imzadi."

Laughs Michael Dorn, who portrays the now lovestruck Klingon, "I think it was a coincidence because I did lobby for it for a long time at conventions. I would talk to the fans and they would love the idea. They really are a cute couple. They are beauty and the beast. It's an interesting triangle because Worf is interested in Troi because of the way she handled his son. He's grown to admire and respect her and, of course, respect is a big thing with Klingons. The thing [rivalry] between Riker and Worf is interesting because they have a great relationship and my line at conventions was that Worf would come up to Commander Riker and say, 'Excuse me, but are you through with Counselor Troi?' After all, you know how guys are."

Frakes, however, has his own designs on the comely Counselor. "Naturally I would like to see it go further," he says. "I'm selfishly interested in their relationship, which I don't think has been explored as completely as it might have been."

Rene Echevarria is more blunt. "I thought if the series is ending, we don't need to have Riker and Troi free to screw space bimbos. So why not have her marry Lieutenant Riker? One of the biggest regrets I have is the impression we've given that time and time again none of the characters is capable of having a genuine relationship. It is something that the fans are aware of and are disappointed by. I think it would have been the right thing to at least bring one of those relationships all the way home."

Marrying Troi and Riker was only one of the many ideas that never made it to the screen seventh season. Several other premises were also vetoed by the executive producers, including an Alexander show which predated 'First Born' in which the young Klingon is transformed into a 25 year old warrior, having lost his childhood.

"There was also a Barclay show called 'Judgment' that was not done," says Brannon Braga. "There was a Q episode that Ron, Rene, Naren and I came up with on our brainstorming trip to Las Vegas in which Q went insane and some of the Enterprise crew found themselves unwittingly in a reality that was completely insane. They come to realize that something's not right, and it turns out that Q has gone insane, and somehow he folded the laws of physics and the universe into his insanity and, in this bizarre reality where different time periods converge, Q is this homeless person going on and on about how he used to be a super being. It was kind of our homage to `The Prisoner' and it didn't get approved. That could have been a classic."

The premise was resurrected for a third season episode of *Deep Space Nine*, "Past Tense" in which Sisko travels back in time to the 21st century.

Other stories included a gay-themed episode in which Wesley becomes romantically entangled with a beautiful alien woman who he later learns changes sex, an Ensign Ro show called "Judgment" in which the murder of a Cardassian is blamed on Ro, a new Moriarty episode in which Sherlock Holmes (and Picard's) arch-nemesis discovers he is trapped in a virtual world and entreats Data to enter with a distress signal, as well as an abortion show that was, er, aborted.

"Michael didn't feel that it worked," says Echevarria. "He was very concerned with it being too pro-life. Though it was ultimately pro-choice, the basic idea we came up with was that we have an alien on the Enterprise that has been on there for years. Some super alien species comes aboard and says 'This is our fetus and it is time to make it either be born into one of us or abort.' The alien never had to feed and never understood why. It took in nutrients through its parents, these energy beings, so there was this dependence and they had the right to terminate the dependence of the fetus. But Michael was concerned that our sympathies would be with the fetus and it would come off as being pro-life, and he is very much pro-choice."

Another approach to

telling an abortion story involved Lal from third season's "The Offspring." Says Echevarria, "It's a show in which Lal's programming is killing Data and he has to choose whether or not to terminate her existence. We would see her on the holodeck and he would tell her, `I have to kill you.' I thought it was great but Michael felt the same way, that the audience's sympathies would be with the metaphorical fetus."

Perhaps of most interest to *Trek* fans was an episode being developed by Naren Shankar to feature Trek *Classic*'s Chekov. "It never went anywhere," says Shankar. "I was working on a Chekov story where he returns as a prisoner-of-war from a planet where he was imprisoned for many years. Now he has come back as an ambassador to help the Federation to open up diplomatic relations, like Vietnam, essentially. The story was going to be about Worf and Chekov because they are both Russian and Worf has heard about him and they kind of strike up a relationship. Throughout the course of the negotiations with these people, it appears as though Chekov is sabotaging them and ultimately it turns out he is essentially plotting to use the Enterprise to lay waste to their capital for revenge and to screw things up

for the Federation because he feels that the Federation abandoned him and let these people torture him."

"I thought that was a very good story," comments Braga. "The idea of Chekov returning and being evil was one that I was quite fond of."

The idea of using a character from the original, once considered anathema, has changed in light of *Next Gen*'s huge popularity. While *TNG* was once considered the bastard child of the original show, viewers have embraced the show so whole-heartedly that the original has become largely overshadowed in their minds. "There were all these dictums that we'll never bring back original cast members or do alternate timelines or time travel shows, and people had sort of forgotten the reasons for those dictums," says Ron Moore of his four year tenure on the show. "The show really began to evolve and by sixth season we were really taking a lot more risks and the show found its strength and just sailed."

The Next Generation had changed dramatically both on-screen and off over its seven years on television, probably most dramatically during its third season. The show's creative team was once best known by the so-called revolving door metaphor used to describe the constant shuf-

fling of writers on and off during the show's first few troubled seasons. "When I first came here, it was legendary," recalls Ron Moore. "Everyone talked about it." Ironically, the final seasons of *Next Gen* have been characterized by stability among the writing staff which has bred a consistent level of quality among the episodes.

Says Moore, "I think the shows have been better. There's more family feeling to the crew, which is reflected because there's more of a family feeling on the staff."

The creative renaissance the show underwent during its pivotal third season is largely attributed to Michael Piller. He had replaced Michael Wagner, after a short tenure, as the head of the writing staff subsequent to the departure of Maurice Hurley, the strong-willed writer/producer who wrote some of the first two season's best episodes while also making enemies of many of the show's staffers.

"I didn't save *Star Trek*," emphasizes Piller. "I think the show would have survived, but I take a great deal of pride in bringing a creative focus to the characters and doing as challenging material as I could help find. I think that we did do some very special things the third and fourth season that set a standard and made the *Next Generation* a must view weekly experience for a lot of people.

"It was Gene Roddenberry's *Star Trek* and it was my job to execute it," says Piller of taking over the show. "You could probably say I wrote almost the whole year third season because the other people here, with the very clear exception of Ira Behr, were so hostile to me and to Gene and they just couldn't find the freedom to write. In the fourth season, I built a staff in the image of what I thought a staff should be. I made it a group of people who really worked together to help one another to make the best show possible. And I think the quality of the show soared. That's my greatest contribution to *Star Trek*."

Despite the continuing series of *Star Trek* feature films and their new responsibilities on the *Trek* spin-offs, most of the creative team that created *TNG* week after week can't help but wax nostalgically over the completion of filming on the series.

"I'll miss the laughter," says Michael Dorn. "I kept telling everyone I'll miss the laughter and the fun we had more than anything else. I never had this much fun on any of the sets that I worked on. But it's not an ending, we'll still have the conventions and the films."

"It was good television which is a rare animal in itself," says Brent Spiner. "I think we satisfied the entertainment angle and, to a large extent, we made allusions to the world we live in. I think we could have been more hard hitting. I think we waffled on a few issues because there were so many rules that were attached to world of *Star Trek*. It would have been nice to break some of those rules and stretch the envelope and go beyond what we did do with this wonderful format."

Recalls Michael Piller, who visited Stage 16 during the final evening of shooting "All Good Things," involving Patrick Stewart and John DeLancie, "The day I went down to say goodbye to Patrick on the stage, I felt a loss. It's the loss I felt from missing a character that I've really become attached to. I think Picard is a remarkable character and Patrick Stewart made him that way. I'm signaling out Patrick because he is a special talent. It's been five years of surprises and delights and you can't imagine how rare it is in television to have the pleasure of working with talents like these people. So I really felt sad the last day when they were shooting the last shot because it was really the perfect teaming of writers and performers where we were able to say something through television in an entertaining fashion."

For others, the significance of the end of the *Next Generation* television era came when they received their invitations to the show's wrap party. A letter which ended with a stark picture of an empty bridge reading 1987 to 1994.

"It was like a funeral notice," says Ron Moore. "You just kind of go, 'Oh man, it's really ending.' And that was the first time it really hit me. Even writing the final episode, it was just a project that we had to get done."

Even former creative consultant Tracy Torme, who predicted when he left the show after the second season that the popularity of *TNG* would never exceed that of the original, has reassessed his feelings about the future of the show. "I think *The Next Generation* will probably be what everyone thinks of when people think of *Star Trek*," he says. "I think given the direction the world is headed in, you're going to see a lot more of *The Next Generation* and a lot less of the old show. It's an unqualified smash success. It's going to live on.

"I haven't seen a whole episode since I left and I watched 'Bloodlines' and the show still has to me a static feel to it," he continues. "It still feels kind of sterile and stiff, which is one reason I thought it may not catch on. I can't really judge it because I haven't watched them, but I have heard good things and I'm going to watch them in repeats. I am kind of surprised because I still feel the old show has more life and is more fun to watch. But I think I'm probably getting to be in the minority in that. *Next Generation* is a very professionally produced show with a great cast and I'm glad I worked on it. I'm proud of my time there and I wouldn't have created my own show if I hadn't been at *Star Trek* first."

"I think the show is going to endure strongly," says Naren Shankar. "It has a fundamental appeal. It gets knocked by a lot of people as being too squeaky clean or optimistic or too unrealistic. I think what many people fail to recognize while taking shots at *Star Trek* is that it is precisely those characteristics that give *Star Trek* its appeal. It is a fundamentally optimistic view of the future that says we can get past our petty foibles and baser instincts and make a better place for ourselves while we're more tolerant, a little more understanding; where violence isn't the only recourse toward solving a problem. Maybe on a subconscious level people respond to that. Maybe that's a large part of the popularity of the show. And there is a lot of

stuff on television you can watch. Some of it's meaningful, some of it less so. If I never work in this industry again, I can look to the years I spent on this show with a certain level of pride and say at least that I was part of it. And that it had a positive effect on people. Hey, if you can say that about your job, then I think you're doing okay."

Indeed, the unprecedented success of *Star Trek* in first run syndication has prompted a renaissance in science-fiction programming both in syndication and on the major broadcast networks.

However, aspiring to *Trek* quality doesn't necessarily make it so. Offers Brannon Braga of a familiar Trekker's appearance on the sci-fi underwater series *seaQuest*, "I thought Shatner did fine, but it was the script. It was this terrible, confusing tech. Even at our worst, our tech does not approach the dolphin's tail wagging through the water creating holographic images."

But can this insatiable hunger for science-fiction programming, and especially *Star Trek*, be satiated? If so, will there be a backlash against the profusion of new genre product in the marketplace? Obviously, nowhere is this concern felt more strongly than behind the hallowed gates of Paramount Pictures

where filming continues on the latest Trek spin-off, *Voyager*.

"We're very aware that there could be a backlash," says Jeri Taylor. "Anything can happen. Somehow, something in me doesn't think that's going to happen. The advance mail that I get and the people that I talk to at conventions are already expressing a great eagerness about *Voyager*. It seems to have excited them. And perhaps it's knowing there will be a starship show out there that has a 'boldly going' feel to it that makes them even more eager to see it. We can only hope for the best and I don't think that, at the moment, the public or our fans' appetite for these kinds of wondrous, imaginative stories has been jaded."

• • • •
EPISODE GUIDE
Season Seven

"Descent, Part II"

"Liaisons"

"Interface"

"Gambit, Part I"

"Gambit, Part II"

"Phantasms"

"Dark Page"

"Attached"

"Force of Nature"

"Inheritance"

"Parallels"

"The Pegasus"

"Homeward"

"Sub Rosa"

"Lower Decks"

"Thine Own Self"

"Masks"

"Eye of the Beholder"

"Genesis"

"Journey's End"

"Firstborn"

"Bloodlines"

"Emergence"

"Preemptive Strike"

"All Good Things"

Episode #153
"Descent, Part II"
Original Airdate: **9/20/93**
Written by **Rene Echevarria**
Directed by **Alexander Singer**
Guest Starring:
Jonathan Del Arco (Hugh), Alex Datcher (Taitt), James Horan (Barnaby), Brian Cousins (Crosis)

As the story continues, Hugh is enraged at the Enterprise crew for their introduction of emotions into him and, in turn, the Borg collective consciousness. This action is what led the way for Lore to become their leader. Despite his anger, he works with Picard to help remove Lore from power, which serves the dual purpose of freeing Data from his brother's maniacal grip. Meanwhile, in space, Crusher is in command of the Enterprise as it engages a Borg warship.

*****

"I don't think it was as good as it could have been," says Brent Spiner, who played both Data and Lore in the episode which was partially filmed on location in Simi Valley at the same synagogue where the Khitomer Conference interiors were filmed for *Star Trek VI*. "There was a real nice potential there, but it was too mammoth of an undertaking on the seven days we're allotted to do shows. There was a nice subtext. Lore wasn't really just

SEASON PREMIERE

TONIGHT AT 7, THE BATTLE YOU'VE WAITED ALL SUMMER TO SEE!

STAR TREK
THE NEXT GENERATION

and Tomorrow at 7,
Season Premiere:
DEEP SPACE NINE

(11)

WPIX

villainous, he believed in what he was doing."

Explains *TNG* Executive Producer Jeri Taylor of the troubled production, "I think that what we found out was that we had too much story to tell. It was such an embarrassment of riches that a lot of

things had to get short shift. The Lore/Data thing took over, forcing us to almost ignore Hugh, who became a very minor kind of character. We were trying to deal with the themes of cults and how a charismatic leader can lure and beguile people. But we had so many themes. Maybe it was just too ambitious because we were not able to do justice to any one of the themes. We spread ourselves so thin and that was our mistake."

"It was like many two-part episodes, there were many balls in the air and late in the process, new balls were added," says Rene Echevarria, who wrote the show. "After the first draft was written, Michael [Piller] became intrigued with the David Koresh angle on Lore, so that needed to be developed. We would have loved to stay on that planet for the entire episode and done Lore, Data and Geordi and our people and all those relationships, but it was unproduceable. We didn't have the sets to keep it from becoming claustrophobic."

Says Brannon Braga of the episode which addressed Data confronting dark emotions brought on by his evil brother, "I think 'Part II' was less successful than 'Part I' in that not enough time was devoted to the relationship between Geordi and Data and Data's experience with these strange, warped, addicting, dark emotions. That was the most interesting part of it. Unfortunately, you had all these disparate elements like Hugh and Riker, and Worf dealing with Hugh, and Beverly as the commander of

the ship which was action and tech. We thought that would sustain the excitement when, in fact, in my opinion, it just served to take away from the more interesting elements. I thought that 'Part I' was better in terms of Data, and his emotional arc, which was all but lost by comparison in 'Part II'. Nevertheless, it was action packed and successful on that level."

As for the future of the malevolent automotons who have made such a mark on the new *Star Trek* series, Braga offers, "The Borg are endlessly fascinating. I have no doubt we'll see them again. In what guise, I don't know."

Episode #154
"Liaisons"
Original Airdate: 9/28/93
Story by **Roger Eschabacher & Jaq Greenspon**
Teleplay by **Jeanne Carrigan Fauci & Lisa Rich**
Directed by **Cliff Bole**
Guest Starring:
Barbara Williams (Anna), Eric Pierpoint (Voval), Paul Eiding (Loquel), Michael Harris (B, 'eth)

Troi, Worf and Picard find themselves manipulated by Lyaaran ambassadors when they agree to partake in a cultural exchange program. Troi's partner, Loquel, is seeking out the more pleasurable aspects of the starship, particularly its

food and drinks. Worf's companion, Byleth, continually provokes the Klingon until he explodes in fury, which actually seems to please the Lyaaran. Picard, having agreed to beam down to the Lyaaran home world, is accidentally stranded on a planet which seems to have one other inhabitant, Anna, who claims to be in love with him while at the same time attempts to hold him captive. Ultimately, it all comes down to the fact that these three aliens have been sent by their people to experience the human emotions of aggression, pleasure and intimacy.

*****

"I was never very excited about this story," admits Brannon Braga, who was saddled with the show's rewrite after the original draft was submitted involving Picard's relationship with an obsessive woman. "When I was in Hawaii writing the movie, I just somehow knew that I was going to get this rewrite. I was dreading it, because I was not a fan of this story. Lisa and Jean's first draft had some very nice things in it, but the relationship wasn't working between Picard and the woman. The woman was a Starfleet woman who was very together and they had a very normal relationship and really did kind a start to be

CINEFANTASTIQUE®

SPECIAL DOUBLE-ISSUE

December 1994

$10.95
CAN $14.50
UK £7.40

STAR TREK
THE NEXT GENERATION

ENDING THE TV VOYAGES

PLUS: DEEP SPACE NINE

STAR TREK: VOYAGER

STAR TREK VII: GENERATIONS

MARY SHELLEY'S FRANKENSTEIN
STARGATE
ROBERT HEINLEIN

Volume 25 Number 6
Volume 26 Number 1

PREVIEW: INTERVIEW WITH THE VAMPIRE

interested in each other. When it turns out that she's actually an alien trying to figure out what love's all about, I had asked the question, 'Well, she did such a good job emulating the human female falling in love, why would they need to learn anything?' What I did was make it a darker story and made the relationship much more sinister and disturbing."

Adds Rene Echevarria, "It was actually pitched very slyly by the writers, who pitched it as kind of a take on *Star Trek*-obsessed fans and that's what made me smile and at least pass it on. What if we did *Misery* with Captain Picard and a big fan of his, and that fell by the wayside. That was just too on the nose and it became something very different."

Jeri Taylor was immediately struck by the pitch when Echevarria passed the premise on to her, "I fell in love with this from the first pitch because it lent itself to something that we had seen work so beautifully in 'Chain of Command II', which is a two-person play with Patrick Stewart. And the idea of a woman who is his captor on a sort of emotional and psychological level seemed, to me, to be fraught with the same kind of dramatic material that we got from 'Chain of

Command.' I think it certainly fulfilled that."

In the early drafts of the script, the show's B story involved Troi's promotion to Commander, a plotline used later in the season for "Thine Own Self."

"The B-line of Troi getting pips was written into the script by Lisa and Jean, who did the first draft and it was a very uneasy marriage," says Taylor. "The stories were not comfortable with each other. We felt that there needed to be something that was more organically linked to the Picard story, and that's when Brannon came up with having the other diplomats from the same race of people. I thought he did an absolutely marvelous job of drawing some very droll, delightful characters who were experiencing our way of life for the first time."

Says Braga, "Troi's commander's test was just working against it from the beginning, so what I did was make it a much darker story and put a twist on it. The relationship became much more sinister and disturbing. We did more of a *Fatal Attraction* thing, which would also more believably dramatize the ambassador's struggle. It suddenly made sense. What you think is a

fatal, twisted obsession at first is really just someone trying to 'get it', which I thought was kind of interesting. Once I got rid of the Troi-Commander arc, I wrote a much more humorous arc with the ambassadors on the ship. Why not use a premise which seemed like something disconnected, but was in fact connected to the main story? Was I happy with the script? Yeah. Was I happy with the episode? I don't know.

"I had a lot of fun writing it, and a lot of it was cut for time, mostly the more fun moments," he adds. "Whether or not they actually ended being funny is another story. It's a matter of opinion. At the end, I give Picard a speech about people who take things to extremes to experience them, and that's what these people do. I thought that was very interesting. In order to understand the culture, you must immerse yourself in that culture. It's still a little scattered, though. In the end, even though it seemed redolent of *Misery* and *Fatal Attraction*, the *Star Trek* twist was, it wasn't at all."

Episode #155
"Interface"
Original Airdate: **10/4/93**
Written by **Joe Menosky**
Directed by **Robert Wiemer**
Guest Starring:
Madge Sinclair (Captain Silva La Forge), Warren Munson (Admiral Holt), Ben Vereen (Doctor La Forge)

Geordi is hooked up to a new virtual reality probe, and while investigating the wreckage of a doomed ship, he discovers his mother onboard after word that she has disappeared arrives from his father. LaForge fails to heed words of warning from Captain Picard and persist sin the experiments in the hopes of saving his mother from death, ultimately learning that the vision is not his mother at all.

*****

Offers Ron Moore of the technobabble-ridden episode written by former *Trek* staffer Joe Menosky, "There's one scene which was a high point of tech for the series, where Joe was trying to explain how the mother was on this ship and it's like Geordi's not really on the ship because he's a probe, but then there's this mother on the ship, but she's not there either, but she might have been in a warp funnel from beaming down to the planet, which is sending a projection to the probe which is going to look like Geordi's

hand. It was this insane world of tech that Joe understood and no one else did. He sits up in the Alps somewhere and just sends this stuff to us."

Adds Naren Shankar, "This show was something that had been around for a while. We had talked about the possibility of doing a show where Riker's father had just passed away and Riker's in this virtual reality program where he goes down to planet and starts seeing images of Alaska. That's what this became eventually. When we realized that it would probably be better to do a story like this with Geordi rather than Riker, we sent it off to Joe immediately and this is what he came back with. To me, it's not real interesting from a gee-wiz standpoint of technology, because we weren't looking at technology four hundred years in the future. I think it's more like forty years into the future. It's almost an overdone type of theme these days. The technology seems out of proportion to the other technologies that we use on the Enterprise."

"It wasn't so much that we hadn't wanted to do it before, we had never quite found a way for the story to work," says Jeri Taylor of the show's virtual reality premise. "It had been pitched two years before as a Riker story and by the time we got around to sort

of working it out, we were at the end of the sixth season and we suddenly had a bunch of Riker stories, so it didn't seem appropriate. We decided to hold it until this year when we realized that its subject matter was very similar to `Frame of Mind' involving Riker and an alternate reality. We had planned the death of Riker's father as something that would have an emotional kind of impact on him, but it just seemed too close to things we had done before. When we came up with the idea of using it for Geordi, everything sort of just broke free and it worked much better."

"We've had the family of everybody else on board," says Taylor. "Every other character has had their family dealt with except Geordi and probably the main reason for doing it was there was an order to finally flesh out his character more than it had been, and to show that he didn't spring isolated from Zeus' forehead."

Another reason for finally depicting Geordi's family was that a long simmering story idea in which it would be established that the ship's chief engineer was the child of aliens had been dropped.

• • • •

"Interface" introduced audiences to Geordi's parents. Actor LeVar Burton is seen here with his wife (photo copyright ©1995 Albert Ortega)

Episode #156
"Gambit, Part I"
Original Airdate: **10/11/93**
Teleplay by **Naren Shankar**
Story by **Chris Hatton and Naren Shankar**
Directed by **Peter Lauritson**
Guest Starring:
Richard Lynch (Baran), Robin Curtis (Tallera), Caitlin Brown (Vekor), Cameron Thor (Narik), Alan Altshuld (Yranac), Bruce Gray (Admiral Chekote).

Riker is abducted by mercenaries who he believes are responsible for killing Captain Picard. Once onboard the alien pirate ship, Riker learns Picard is still alive and passing himself off as Gaylen, one of the smugglers, who are searching for a rare artifact. Meanwhile, Riker tries to convince the smugglers he has turned his back on Starfleet and is going to join them.

*****

The show is referred to jokingly on staff as the "yo ho, ho, pirate show," a concept that had long been considered anathema on *TNG*. "I read the script and I was not particularly taken with it when Michael [Piller] gave it to me last season," recalls Jeri Taylor. "And then I kind of put the script aside and four months later I wrote Michael a memo which said something like, 'Although I wasn't fond of this story, rather like a hen who sits on her eggs for a long time, I've

become attached to it and the more I thought about it I could just sort of say, maybe this could work.' It ended up sort of working so well that we made two parts out of it and, yes, it's a pirate story. But I think that it was romp."

Writer Naren Shankar's original idea for the xenophobic Vulcan isolationist movement featured in the story was that they were literally planning to phase the planet out of our universe to avoid cultural contamination from alien species. "Everyone was afraid it was going to be like a *Space: 1999* episode," says Shankar. "The notion was to dimensionally shift the planet so you couldn't get to them. In that sense, it would be pure isolation. I still think that's a cool idea. Nobody else does, however."

"I was never very enthused about 'Gambit,'" says Brannon Braga. "When the story was purchased, I thought it was not attracted to the campy, swashbuckling elements and was afraid it would just look very corny. I don't think we do campiness very well — especially, in the way we tried to do it with 'Gambit.' It came off like *Buck Rogers: The Series* and why do that? Is that good? We try many different mediums. I was curious as to why we were involving ourselves in a medium that is not

usually a respected one."

Star Trek III's Robin Curtis plays a Vulcan isolationist in the episode, the villainous Tallera.

Episode #157
"Gambit, Part II"
Original Airdate: **10/18/94**
Teleplay by **Ronald D. Moore**
Story by **Naren Shankar**
Directed by **Alexander Singer**
Guest Starring:
Richard Lynch (Baran), Robin Curtis (Tallera), Caitlin Brown (Vekor), Cameron Thor (Narik), James Worthy (Koral), Sabrina LeBeauf (Ensign Giusti)

Picard learns that the pirates are seeking a psionic resonator, a mystical device of unspeakable power from Vulcan history. Once they have obtained the location of the resonator, Picard learns that Tallera is actually a Vulcan operative, but an isolationist who is determined to prevent alien intrusions on the planet Vulcan.

*****

"I felt we ran out of story in 'Part II,'" says writer Ron Moore. "There were places where I was treading water. We had to find the lost ark and I didn't know what the lost ark was. Instead, we had a device from ancient Vulcan myth that had mythic properties that you explain are telepathic focusing properties. I was trying really hard

Captain Picard as a pirate? That was the premise of "Gambit" (Patrick Stewart photograph copyright ©1995 Albert Ortega).

to make this thing work and in the end, I just said 'All right, maybe we should just go for it and make this a classic Gene [Roddenberry] kind of message and go for 'think happy thoughts' and make it something which tied into the backstory of Vulcan and of Surak and peace. I thought it would fit in nicely. I'm not sure if it did. It might have just fallen in on its own gooiness."

Starring in the episode as the show's villain was Richard Lynch playing Baran. Of course, playing a genre baddie for Lynch is nothing new, he's a familiar staple of sci-fi TV having appeared in episodes of *Battlestar Galactica*, *Buck Rogers* and countless low-budget horror films. "Richard was simply the best person who read for the part," says Jeri Taylor. "[Producer] Peter Lauritson, who directed the first episode, knew his work, liked him and really wanted him. It's always a problem to find worthy adversaries for Picard. You need an actor who has the power, stature and presence to go toe to toe with him and if you don't have that, you don't have an episode. Richard brought all of this and for his campiness and the sort of his stereotypical things that he has done, he has that undeniable power and I thought that it was a good trade."

Another casting coup

for the episode was a guest appearance by Los Angeles Laker James Worthy as an imposing, foul Klingon warrior. The famous Laker basketball star underwent a prosthetic transformation into the tallest Klingon in the galaxy for "Gambit, Part II" as a Klingon mercenary whose craft is intercepted by the Enterprise.

"He called Rick and said he wanted to do *Star Trek* and they had lunch and Rick let me know that he was interested in doing the show," says Jeri Taylor. "So when we did 'Gambit' we developed this part and I told Rick who said 'Wait a minute, I didn't say give him a part. He's a basketball player. I don't know if he can act.' But I thought Worthy did a terrific job. He understood this person. He had presence and he had an arrogance. He just stepped right into the part and did an excellent job."

Episode #158
"Phantasms"
Original Airdate: **10/25/93**
Written by **Brannon Braga**
Directed by **Patrick Stewart**
Guest Starring:
Gina Ravarra (Ensign Tyler), Bernard Kates (Sigmund Freud), Clyde Kusatsu (Admiral Nakamura), David L. Crowley (Workman)

When Data begins experiencing some frightening nightmares, including one in

which he is disassembled by miners, he realizes that his nightmare images may hold the clue to a parasitic invasion of the ship which could result in the death of the crew.

*****

One of the episode's most effective images in the episode is Data's vision of Troi transformed into a cake in Ten Forward. "Troi as a cake got the most fevered response from the art department of anything that we have ever done in the four years that I have been here," laughs Jeri Taylor. "They were so disturbed and concerned about this that the entire department stayed after the production of it to implore us not to do this. Brannon and I were somewhat mystified by this because we didn't see it as that big a problem. Brannon had shot a student film in which he had done something very similar and for a $1.98 and had managed to bring it off. Then he found a rock video that had a similar kind of thing and we were just sure that it could work. The only problem was that Patrick [Stewart], who directed it, shot one angle that we had expressly told him not to shoot and it made it very clear that it was someone's neck coming out of a cake."

Offers Producer David Livingston, "The writers can write this stuff, but sometimes

when we do it in production, it's really hard to pull off. What we lack is R&D time and it always astounds me how the crafts people on this show are able to pull these gags off. I thought that 'Phantasms' did it really well and Patrick did a terrific job on the episode."

Where do these surreal dream images come from? Braga speculates, "I could say something clever like I've always wanted to see somebody eat Counselor Troi, but the truth is those kinds of images perhaps are all most attractive to me because I don't understand where they come from. I see the value in darker imagery, more bizarre imagery and what was especially fun about putting them in the *Star Trek* universe is they're such an incongruous juxtaposition to what people expect from the *Next Generation,* which is a somewhat sterile, reality-based universe. So, when suddenly you got these kind of completely disarming and disturbing images, it works."

The idea of portraying Data's nightmares was not new. Braga had first gotten the premise when he gave Data dreams in sixth season's "Birthright" two-parter. "It wasn't until I came up with the idea of creatures that only Data could subliminally perceive, because of his positronic brain, that I got the story. It was a blast to do and it was a pure pleasure to write."

Braga even got to create a scene in which Data seeks counseling from Sigmund Freud himself, the groundbreaking psychoanalyst who has proven a source of great fascination for Braga over the years. "I've wanted to dig my claws in for a long time and really undermine the Freudian concepts that have pervaded the American cultural mainstream and are so much a part of therapy and self-help therapy," he says. "The basic Freudian concepts of the subconscious ego and all the other terms have become a given in the way people think about the way the mind works in America. But, why? How do we know that's how it works? How do we know any of that stuff is true? It's probably not, and you're seeing a huge backlash starting with Freud. Is the Freud dead movement? I'm happy to have been one of the first to comment on it.

"Don't get me wrong," he elaborates. "Freud is the most fun of all the group psychologists. I'm a huge fan. Do I think his theory is incredible? Who am I to say? I certainly would like to think there's a subconscious. I don't know. I'm more a fan of Jung when it comes to what's really going on, but who's to say? The interesting thing is when you look at the episode, it is completely Freudian. The premise of the show is Freudian, Data's subconscious mind. The way in which images manifest themselves in his dreams. It's all Freudian mechanisms so at the same time that I was discrediting Freud in the episode,

I was using all of his concepts to explain everything. To be honest, it's something I definitely think about because it's not helping people break out of their mindsets about the Freudian concepts in this culture when they're seeing it portrayed in the 24th Century as a given; that that is the way the mind works. It's not until shows start showing different ways in which the mind works that you are going to get people breaking free of their Freudian concepts — so there's a tremendous contradiction in the episode in that regard."

Episode #159
"Dark Page"
Original Airdate: **11/1/93**
Written by **Hilary J. Bader**
Directed by **Les Landau**
Guest Starring:
Majel Barrett (Lwaxana Troi), Norman Large (Maques), Kirsten Dunst (Hedril), Amick Byram (Mr. Troi)

Troi is forced to enter her mother's metaconscious mind to discover the hidden trauma which is killing Lwaxana. With the help of an alien delegate, Maques, who forments the bonding, Troi begins to explore inside Mrs. Troi's mind. At the same time, Lwaxana is trying to prevent her daughter from learning that her youngest daughter, who Deanna never knew, drowned when she was very young.

"Dark Page" managed to provide a little more background on Deanna Troi (Marina Sirtis, seen here with her husband) (photo copyright ©1995 Albert Ortega)

*****

"There was a great reluctance to do this episode and 'Phantasms' back to back, but it was one of those predicaments where we didn't have anything else ready to go," says Jeri Taylor. "'Dark Page' had been around a long, long time and it had undergone many permutations. Hillary Bader had pitched this story and it just never seemed to work. It started as a Dr. Crusher story and went through every possible combination of people on the Enterprise. It wasn't until we hit upon Troi and Mrs. Troi that it really seemed to work, and then it was a long time before we could figure out what the secret was that is hurting Mrs. Troi. Ultimately, I think it worked really well and was an emotional episode. It provided a depth to Mrs. Troi's character that we had not seen before."

Brannon Braga, who was writing "Phantasms" at the same time the writers were breaking "Dark Page," was less enthused about the show. "I was dying to write 'Dark Page' and I couldn't for timing reasons," he says. "I thought it was just a great premise that Bader gave us to dip into with the counselor exploring the psyche of her mother and finding out that it's a dark and scary place. It's is a great idea. But, I was thinking, 'You can't do this one. I want to do this in "Phantasms." You guys are killing me."

"I think Rene, who did the production re-write on the episode, did a magnificent job on the show," says Naren Shankar. "It's sort of like *The Joy Luck Club*. It was better than I expected. It was quite touching in many ways."

Episode #160
"Attached"
Original Airdate: **11/8/93**
Written by **Nicholas Sagan**
Directed by **Jonathan Frakes**
Guest Starring:
Robin Gammell (Mauric), Lenore Kasdorf (Lorin)

Picard and Dr. Crusher are kidnapped, and through a telepathic link discover their true feelings for each other while two feuding races, so distrustful of each other and the Federation, have their dispute mediated by a befuddled Commander Riker.

*****

Nicholas Sagan, a television and interactive game writer, admits that many of his early pitches for the show were off-base. "I was a little naive," he laughs. "I was trying to do things they wouldn't have wanted me to do. I did one story involving Charlie X from the original *Star Trek* and another which brought back Armis from 'Skin of Evil.'"

Ultimately it was a pitch that Sagan made involving a physical link ala *The Defiant Ones* between Picard and Dr. Crusher that intrigued the writing staff, but a long simmering resistance to explore their relationship had to be overcome before the story was given the go-ahead.

"I believe the actors wanted it, the fans wanted it, the writing staff wanted it, but

it was just the very top guys who felt that everything should be done with looks and suggestions and let the audience assume what they wanted from that," says Sagan.

Offers Ron Moore of the blossoming of the Picard/Crusher romance, "There was a real hesitancy of whether we should say any of the stuff up front or whether it should be all subtext. I thought, let's just do it and stop toying around with this non-existent relationship. I wanted to do something that explained how he felt and why he never acted on it."

In the story break for the episode, Picard and Crusher kiss when they find themselves as fugitives on the alien planet. Everyone knew selling the plot point to producer Michael Piller would be the challenge. Mapping the story out on the familiar dry erase board, Sagan bowed out to veteran producer Ron Moore who began outlining the episode for Piller. "I didn't need to be up there and Ron's very good at going through the board," says Sagan. "He explained, 'We have this planet and they're talking and then they kiss.' Michael, who had been sort of quiet but into the story, paused and looked at us and said 'Absolutely not.' Instead, it became this very touching scene that's in there

The Picard-Crusher relationship was dealt with for the first time in years in "Attached" (Patrick Stewart and Gates McFadden photograph copyright ©1995 Albert Ortega).

now where Picard's keeping her warm and it's the most poignant and memorable moment in the entire episode."

Agrees Jonathan Frakes, who directed the episode, "We finally saw Picard and Crusher together and I thought it was great. I particularly liked the long scene of them together by the campfire where they really explored their relationship and their attraction to each other."

"We didn't consciously want to wrap up arcs or bring things to neat conclusions because, of course, the feature film series will continue so we didn't want that sense that we had sewn things nicely into a box," says Jeri Taylor. "We simply wanted to tell good, provocative, interesting stories about our people. Nick Sagan had pitched the premise originally about Beverly and Picard being linked together physically and I thought that that gave us great dramatic possibility. Michael was not so sure and then we got another pitch of them being linked telepathically and it was the combination of the two that kind of put it over the edge. So we had to sort of overcome that hurdle first. Then it's the question of how far do you go? How much do you push this? What do you say? What do you not say? Where do you leave it? It was a tightrope act every step of the way. I think the fans uni-versally liked this episode up until the last scene and then many, many of them felt very cheated. There's a very vocal group out there that wants this to be explored even more and have them get married. To us, that's not been the right way to go. Patrick doesn't feel that Jean Luc Picard would move in that direction. I think all of us in the decision making ranks feel that that's not the thing to do and so it was fine to tell a delicate story of unspoken feelings, but to have taken it any further than that would have been wrong."

Sagan notes that the final scene — in which Beverly rebuffs Picard, entreating him that they should just remain close friends — was one of the most important scenes of the show. "I wanted to make the ending as heart breaking as possible," he says. "I heard criticism of the episode from fans who said what was the point of the episode if they didn't actually get together, and I think that's really missing the point. It's really about people who make choices that prevent them from getting together...or at least from getting married. I think there's something kind of touching about the inability of that to happen."

"I think Picard was shocked and very dismayed," comments Patrick Stewart. "I think it took a long time for him to get to the point where he could make that proposal, and I think with customary male vanity he was a little surprised."

"That was really terrific," Gates McFadden enthuses. "I think Jeri Taylor has always been in agreement that we should do something with Dr. Crusher and Picard and pick up that thread again, which all the fans who write Patrick and me want to see. We've got so many letters asking what happened to their relationship. I thought the episode was terrific because it doesn't close the door at all."

Episode #161
"Force of Nature"
Original Airdate: **11/15/93**
Written by **Naren Shankar**
Directed by **Robert Lederman**
Guest Starring:
Michael Corbett (Rabal), Margaret Reed (Serova), Lee Arenberg (Prak)
A pair of alien scientists attempt to warn the Enterprise crew about the dangers of warp drive to the fabric of sub-space in their sector, while the Enterprise is engaged in the rescue of a missing Federation vessel. Ultimately, the Enterprise crew discovers that the use of warp drive is having a detrimental effect on space and warp limits are imposed on all Federation starships on non-emergency business.

*****

"I think this is the worst show that I collaborated on this season," says Michael Piller. "It certainly inspired us to have several meetings on where the season was going because I felt we were letting it slip away."

"There were preposterous moments in that show," says Brannon Braga. "On the other hand, we knew the risks, but we felt it was real important to at least try to do an environmental show. We struggled with making it a personal story and in the end it just didn't work as well as we wanted it to. We couldn't find a personal angle. When you limit warp drive, the rug is being pulled out from under *Star Trek*. I wish more time had been spent with that, and less time with Spot and Cat."

The genesis of the show, once known as 'Limits,' was in a story idea devised by Joe Menosky who was attempting to craft an allegory for contemporary environmental problems. Yet when Braga told Menosky that the staff was going ahead with the story, Braga relates, "He said, 'Are you crazy? Are you out of your minds?' The reason we'd been avoiding it was because we were afraid it would get preachy and techy and, unfortunately, it

was both."

Explains Naren Shankar of the tenuous link between the show's A story and a B story involving Data training his cat, Spot, "The slightest dramatic connection between those two is the notion that you can't control a force of nature like a cat."

"This was a troubled episode from the first," says Jeri Taylor. "It was a wonderful environmental premise that something we take for granted is doing damage to the space around us. It was the metaphor which most closely evoked our present situation. We had tried it in many guises and it never worked. At the beginning of the seventh year, I sent Naren and Brannon to a big breakfast meeting of an environmental watchdog group that we have here in Hollywood and they came back inspired. Naren was so galvanized. He said, 'I want to take a crack at "Limits." I want to do this. This is important.' I agreed. It was a story I really wanted to do and I think it does make an important statement, but dramatizing a huge issue like that is always the trouble. We started down many roads. At first, we had Geordi's sister come on board to help him adjust to the death of his mother [in 'Interface'], but that seemed to muddle every-

thing completely. We then started the whole little thread of Geordi in competition with the engineer from another ship so that we could show Geordi's deeply felt belief in technology and the benefits of technology, so that he would be at war with himself when realizing that it was contributing to something disastrous.

"When the script was written," she adds, "it turned out to be very, very short and so we then started adding scenes about Data's cat. By luck, or by bad luck, all of those scenes turned out to be at the beginning of the show, so you had an episode that started very fitfully and seemed to be about Data's Cat and then it took a turn and seemed to be about Geordi and his rivalry with this other guy. Then it went back to the cat and then, finally, in about the third act, the real story began and, by that point, I think people were hopelessly lost. It sort of never got back on track, but it's still an important idea and our intentions were good."

Data was reunited with his "mother" for the first time in "Inheritance" (Brent Spiner photograph copyright ©1995 Albert Ortega).

Episode #162
"Inheritance"
Original Airdate: **11/22/93**
Teleplay by **Dan Koeppel and Rene Echevarria**
Story by **Dan Koeppel**
Directed by **Robert Scheerer**
Guest Starring:
Fionnula Flanagan (Juliana), William Lithgow (Pran)

Data learns that a scientist exploring seismic activity on Atrea may be his "mother," the wife of the late Doctor Noonian Soong. At first Data is reluctant to believe her, but in a startling revelation discover she is not his mother, but an android built before him. After an accident, which reveals this fact, Data chooses to keep the fact she is an android from her so that she can continue to live a normal life.

*****

"'Inheritance' came to us as a pitch the previous season and Michael's comment at the time was that it doesn't seem like there's enough here to make a story," says Jeri Taylor. "It's an example of a situation in which he was more trusting of us to be able to take a somewhat slender premise and develop it. We went for the emotional part of it, which was Data and his relationship with his mother."

Adds Rene Echevarria, "I loved the pitch when I heard it. I really wanted to write it. I loved Fionnula Flanagan. She just did a wonderful job and was magic. I really poured myself into it and much to my disappointment, I watched it with my wife thinking that she would love it, but she's just not a Data fan and she just couldn't invest herself in it."

"I liked the idea," says Brannon Braga. "I thought it was, for those who weren't party to the story, a shock when you find out she's an android. I just thought it was very well written. I liked their relationship and, ultimately, I just was kind of very intrigued by the moral dilemmas involved. I thought Data's solution was very surprising and thought it turned out great."

Actress Fionnula Flanagan, who plays Juliana, had already appeared in an episode of *Deep Space Nine* the same season, which made her casting problematic. "She came in and read and just knocked everybody out with her reading," says Jeri Taylor. "But there was some fear that she would be recognizable [from *DS9*] and that we're sort of shattering the curtain of disbelief if you see the same person in a couple of episodes playing a different role. It calls attention to the fact that it's an actor, not a character. However, we looked at her film from *Deep Space Nine* and she was an alien and was very different, so we felt the two roles would be far enough apart and I'm glad it worked out that way, because now it's hard to imagine anyone else having done it."

Episode #163
"Parallels"
Original Airdate: **11/29/93**
Written by **Brannon Braga**
Directed by **Robert Wiemer**
Guest Starring:
Wil Wheaton (Wesley Crusher), Patti Yasutake (Ogawa), Mark Bramhall (Gul Nador)

Returning home from a bat'telh tournament, Worf finds himself experiencing several alternate realities aboard the Enterprise, including one in which he is married to Counselor Troi. After Data learns that a flaw in Geordi's VISOR has expanded a rift in realities, an attempt is made to return Worf to his own reality, which leads to an infinite number of converging universes, including one in which the Federation is losing a war with the Borg. Despite their attempt to stop Worf from returning to his own universe, he is finally successful.

*****

"It began as a Picard story," says Brannon Braga, who notes that it had originally been planned that Tasha Yar would exist in the alternate realities Worf experienced, but it was decided that would make the episode appear to be

Worf (Michael Dorn) finds himself slipping in and out of different dimensions in "Parallels"
(photograph copyright ©1995 Albert Ortega)

too similar to "Yesterday's Enterprise." As a result, Wesley was substituted instead. "What we also realized when we were breaking it was that there's just not a lot of personal stuff that you could do with Picard that would be different in alternate realties, so we decided to make it the Worf story and go through the Worf/Troi romance. It's fascinating. I don't think most people expected it. Viewers who watched closely will see that we've been building their relationship for the past couple of years. Wesley could have been explored in more depth, but I thought it would just be more interesting if he were just there. There was a temptation to do something, but again, I wanted to throw more attention to the Troi/Worf story and having Troi realize that there were realities where Worf never loved her, which is something we all think about. What if's in our relationships."

Opines Jeri Taylor, "I remember when Brannon wrote me the memo in which he sort of outlined this premise. I thought, 'This could be great but it could be very confusing.' I gave the memo to Michael and he wrote back and said 'Okay. Good luck on the break.' I think it was a measure of his trust that on the basis of just a memo outlining what was clearly a potentially very confusing, elaborate premise that we turned it into a cohesive story that worked like gangbusters. It was not the intention when we started breaking it that the story would be Worf and Troi. That was a curious little sideline in one of the realities. Later, as the season developed, we began to develop the notion a little more strongly that Worf had been thinking about her ever since his experience in 'Parallels.'"

In fact, the Worf/Troi romance was a subplot that had been brewing since fifth season's "Ethics" in which Worf is paralyzed after an accident in the cargo bay. "In 'Fistful of Datas' there was an effort to gradually bring Worf and Troi a little closer," says Taylor. "It would have happened through Alexander that she began giving him advice about him and functioned as a surrogate mother. That kind of thing is without conscious design. It just sort of erupted into bloom at the end of the last season and I think has given us some very nice moments."

In writing the episode, Brannon Braga needed to avoid playing many of the same beats as in the previous season's "Frame of Mind" in which Riker confronts a reality that is apparently breaking down before him.

"If you watch this episode you'll see that people are wondering, and Worf himself is wondering, whether he's losing his mind, because of a head injury," says Braga. "That's an element I had to be aware to play down because then you would be stepping in 'Frame of Mind' territory, 'Am I going crazy?'"

Episode #164
"The Pegasus"
Original Airdate: 1/10/94
Written by **Ronald D. Moore**
Directed by **LeVar Burton**
Guest Starring:
Nancy Vawter (Admiral Blackwell), Terry O' Quinn (Admiral Pressman)

The Enterprise goes in search of a missing starship that vanished 12 years earlier while conducting a mysterious experiment. The ship had been captained by Admiral Pressman, with Riker as a member of his bridge crew.

Riker's loyalties are tested when he must violate Pressman's admonitions and reveal to Picard that they are looking for an illegally tested phasing cloaking device, which the Enterprise eventually uses to escape from being trapped inside an asteroid when the Romulans try to sabotage their salvage efforts.

*****

"It started with my notion of doing *Raise The*

Riker (Jonathan Frakes) is reunited with his first captain in "The Pegasus," and together they engage in a covert operation (photo copyright ©1995 Albert Ortega).

Titanic," says Ron Moore of the Clive Cussler book in which the Titanic is covertly salvaged for its secret cargo. "I wanted to do a story about a mystery ship from a long time ago that holds a secret within. It's a classic sort of tale and right from the get go I thought maybe Riker could have been on that ship. What is he protecting?"

Terry O'Quinn, who gives a commanding performance as Admiral Pressman, earns universal kudos from the staff and Michael Piller suggests he could be resurrected for a future episode of *Deep Space Nine*. "It was a gift that we got him," says Jeri Taylor. "He was in town heading home to Baltimore and we hurried over to read him an hour before he was supposed to catch his plane. We lucked out in that this is one of Ron's finest pieces of writing. It's action adventure but with a moral tale at the core, and that's what made this episode one of the best of the season, I think. The story of Riker's moral dilemma was explored beautifully and it was just one of those *Star Trek*'s that's everything *Star Trek* should be."

"I am proud to say that I've written another insane Admiral," laughs Ron Moore. "They must put something in the water at Federation Headquarters. The episode

also started with one of my most insane ideas. It began with Data, Troi and Riker rehearsing *Pygmalion* and I was using Data's learning about acting as some kind of metaphor for improvising, and it later became a way of talking to Riker. Everybody read the scene and said 'I really like the script, but what is this *Pygmalion* stuff?'"

Episode #165
"Homeward"
Original Airdate: **1/17/94**
Teleplay by **Naren Shankar**
Story by **Spike Steingasser**
Directed by **Alexander Singer**
Guest Starring:
Penny Johnson (Dobara), Brian Markinson (Vorin), Edward Penn (Kateras), Paul Sorvino (Nikolai)

Worf's foster brother, Nikolai, violates the Prime Directive in attempting to save remnants of a dying race, prompting a heated discussion of Prime Directive issues among the senior staff. Rebuffing Picard's orders, Nikolai attempts to recreate the village of the dying race in the holodeck in order to transport the survivors to a new world without them discovering what has happened.

*****

"I thought it was a pretty good show," says Michael Piller. "Paul Sorvino gave a very good performance and I think

the only thing for me is that I felt a little shortchanged between Worf and his brother. Somehow their relationship never quite had a depth to it, it seemed by the numbers to me."

The show uneasily combines two separate premises and featured good fella Paul Sorvino as Worf's brother. "We constantly get rumors of feature actors and stars who want to do *Star Trek*. We have spent days following up on these rumors only to find that usually they're not true or even if they're true, the people aren't available," says Jeri Taylor. "It's been an exercise in futility. Paul Sorvino called, asked for an appointment with me, came to my office, sat down and said 'I love this series, I want to do something on it. I'm serious. Please believe me. I will be available to you.' So when the story about Worf's brother came along, I thought well, let's see if this man is going to back that up. We called him and he was on board in an instant. I was really thrilled because I thought he brought a great, great presence to the story."

The series in its last few years has eschewed prime directive stories such as second year's "Pen Pals", but in "Homeward" the Federation non-intervention prohibition plays a key role in preventing Picard from helping the doomed Boraalans. "I have problems with the prime directive as it stands," affirms Ron Moore. "I'm sort of the anti-prime directive staff writer which is just the same as a heretic. I was rooting for Worf's brother the whole time. I thought this guy was right and our people are just letting these guys fry. I always thought the prime directive was a little more flexible than the way it gets portrayed on the show."

"It was a pairing of premises," says Taylor. "Rene [Echevarria] came to me one day and said that he had gotten a pitch about the idea of transporting people from a dying world onto the holodeck and fooling them into thinking they were still there. I said Rene, `Are you crazy? That's not even credible. Get out of here.' So about a month later he came back and said, 'I've been thinking about that tribe on the holodeck' and I said, 'Why are you bringing that up? I don't want to hear that. Go away.' So he just kind of kept hanging in there with it and I could never see it and never see it and then about that time we got the pitch about Worf's human brother, who we had never heard anything about. Rene said, 'I was thinking that might be a good way to tell the story of the tribe on the holodeck.' So I finally started thinking about it and thought,

well all right. Maybe I overreacted. Maybe it could work. So I memoed Michael and he approved it. It turned out to be a really strong idea."

Episode #166
"Sub Rosa"
Original Airdate: **1/31/94**
Written by **Brannon Braga**
Directed by **Jonathan Frakes**
Guest Starring:
Michael Keenan (Maturin), Shay Duffin (Ned Quint), Duncan Regehr (Ronin)

While attending the funeral of her grandmother on a planet which was terraformed to resemble Glasgow, Scotland, Dr. Crusher experiences visions of the ghost she learns has haunted her family for generations. Meanwhile, Geordi and Data attempt to repair the planet's weather control grid while Picard tries to convince Dr. Crusher to remain with Starfleet when she abruptly hands in her resignation to join Ronin back on the planet. It is only when Picard reveals that he is an apparition metaphasic energy that Ronin's spell is broken and Crusher phasers him out of existence.

*****

There are few episodes on which viewers' opinions are more divided than "Sub Rosa." Those who enjoyed the show and those who despised *Trek's* first foray into the genre of gothic horror can be sepa-

rated largely across gender lines. In other words, men hate it, women love it.

"I can still reduce Brannon to shudders when I go into his office and say 'I can travel on the power transfer beam,'" laughs Rene Echevarria, who was initially wary of doing the episode. "But the cast loved it. Every woman on the lot who read it was coming up to Brannon and patting him. Ultimately I think it was worth doing because it was campy fun and the production values were wonderful. The sets look great and everybody threw themselves into it. Gates did a wonderful job. It just got bigger and bigger and broader and broader and to the point of grandmother leaping out of the grave. Just having Beverly basically writhing around having an orgasm at 6 o'clock on family TV was great. For that alone it was worth doing. We got away with murder."

"It came as a pitch from a freelance writer," says Jeri Taylor. "The original spec script was that there have been aliens throughout history on Earth who had possessed people and they was responsible for much of what we called supernatural paranormal events. She had the idea of the Scottish kind of origins of Beverly. Rick and Michael were very distrustful of this story. They considered it a romance novel in space and felt the possibility for embarrassment was monumental, but I just knew it would work. It's a different kind of story for *Star Trek* to tell. It is a romance but we do have women in our audience and women do traditionally respond to romantic stories. Myself being one of them. One of Brannon and my favorite movies is *The Innocence*, which comes from Henry James' *Turn of the Screw*. We saw this episode as an homage, and we packed in every sort of gothic ghost story trick that one could imagine."

Says Brannon Braga, "I always loved the idea of a ghost that hangs around the grounds, having sex with the mortals. 'Sub Rosa' was a blast to do. It was exciting to take the gothic horror genre and somehow make it *Star Trek* and, I thought that was a lot of fun."

Not everyone agreed. Naren Shankar recalls being one of the story's early opponents. "It's a gothic ghost story," he says. "Either you buy it or you don't buy it at all, and I was sort of in the latter category."

Despite some early reluctance on staff, the show went forward and proved one of the best vehicles for Gates McFadden of the series' seven year run. "It was the best performance I've ever seen," says Braga. "I just thought she did a wonderful job. Picard catches Beverly masturbating, for crying out loud. What a tough role to play. When I was writing the words, 'She writhes around in the bed' having invisible sex, I just thought, 'Oh, man, we're asking for trouble. Are they gonna be able to pull this off?' Thanks to [director] Jonathan Frakes and Gates, it was not hokey. It was very good."

"Look, I scripted the first orgasm in `The Game,'" he adds. "This was mild by comparison. Sure, it was racy. Even Rick Berman had said, 'I can't believe we're doing this.' I think they trimmed quite a bit out of the writhing sequences."

Offers Frakes, who embraced directing this offbeat *Trek* installment, "I drew a good straw because it wasn't a *Star Trek*. It was more like *Tales From The Crypt*. Gates and I have worked well together and she has never was better than in 'Sub Rosa' and never looked more beautiful. She looked like a movie star."

The title itself is inspired by Greek myth about a god who was trying to hide a love affair from Cupid. Sub Rosa is Latin for "under the rose," which referred to a secret love affair which is exactly what Beverly Crusher was having in the episode.

Episode #167
"Lower Decks"
Original Airdate: 2/7/94
Teleplay by **Rene Echevarria**
Story by **Ronald Wilkerson and Jean-Louise Matthias**
Directed by **Gabrielle Beaumont**

An episode that focuses on life aboard the Enterprise for several young officers who become involved with a secret mission to return a Cardassian spy across enemy lines.

*****

"I tried to keep our people in it," says Rene Echevarria. "I wanted to pair each one of the characters with one of our characters, so there was some kind of relationship going on with all of them. The idea was to see our people, and a mission, through the eyes of these younger people. To me, this episode was the most joy to write. Basically, I turned in the first draft and with the exception of the fifth act, everything was filmed as I wrote it, which was very satisfying."

As a result of the show running short, additional dialogue was added between Nurse Ogawa and Dr. Crusher. "I thought the show was one of the best ideas we've have had in quite awhile," says Ron Moore. "It was a really unique concept. There was a debate early on about how much it was going to be their show and how much it was going to

impression, to say the least. "I don't know how that rumor got started," says Taylor. "It was just a rampant rumor that would not die. I am just mystified as to why people thought that three middle age people — Rick, Michael and myself — would ever create a series that had nothing but a bunch of young *90210* people on it. It was just absolutely out of the question. The episode was a wonderful premise from Ron Wilkerson and Jean Matthias. who have given us other wonderful premises and a beautiful script with 'Lessons.' Unfortunately, we were in a time bind. I had to have a staff member do it, so Rene took it over and wrote a wildly off concept show, but that's what made it work. It was how does the Enterprise look to those little junior officers who don't get to go into the observation lounge and who don't know what's going on? It was just a really fresh, original idea and I think as it turned out, one of the best episodes of the season."

One of the show's most appealing characters was that of Ensign Sito, played by Sharon Fill, reprising her role from fifth season's "The First Duty."

"In the early drafts of the script, we left her death somewhat ambiguous because we thought we might pull her back in to help us out in some stories that were happening further on down the road," says Taylor. "When I mentioned that to Michael, he said, 'Absolutely not, she's dead. She stays dead. That would undermine the whole episode.' So I said fine. The morning after Michael saw the episode, he came in and said, 'We can't let her stay dead. We've got to bring her back. She was wonderful.' He was really bowled over by the episode."

Before you could say "only Vulcans have a katra," Piller already had a *Deep Space Nine* story in development for the character. When asked about *Trek*'s penchant for reviving its dead, "Sarek didn't come back," Piller retorts. " We received very insightful, intelligent letters that said that *Star Trek* is about hope and optimism and you broke all of our hearts,' which is exactly what I wanted to hear on one level. But I also listen to that. I think that the character was so good, and Jeri in her wisdom allowed there to be a loophole, and we got some very good ideas of why it will be successful to bring her back."

be our show. Ultimately, Michael said this is their show, which I thought was a good decision — especially since he usually says it has to be about our characters — which is what made the show so good."

Many viewers thought the episode was a backdoor pilot for *Voyager*, a mistaken

Episode #168
"Thine Own Self"
Original Airdate: **2/14/94**
Teleplay by **Ronald D. Moore**
Story by **Christopher Hatton**
Directed by **Winrich Kolbe**
Guest Starring:
Ronnie Clare Edwards (Talur), Kimberly Callum (Gia), Andy Kossin (Apprentice), Richard Miro (Rainer), Michael G. Hagerty (Kural), Michael Rothhar (Donnell)

An amnesiac Data is stranded on an alien world after his shuttlecraft crashes while carrying dangerously radioactive material, which is adversely affecting the residents of a village. Back on the Enterprise, Troi studies to take her Commander's test under the tutelage of a less-than-understanding Riker.

*****

"The story came as a pitch from Christopher Hatton, who had written the spec script from which 'Gambit' came," says Jeri Taylor. "He was a young college student in Iowa and as soon as he had sold his premise to 'Gambit,' he came out here and said 'I want to be a writer. I want to pitch you some more ideas.' And my heart kind of sank because he didn't realize how difficult it is to pitch stories and that lightning wasn't going to strike twice. But sure enough, he came in to pitch with the idea of Data as

Frankenstein, which was just irresistible."

Of course, having the show take place on a planet required that a shipboard B story be written to balance the elaborate production requirements necessitated by building an alien civilization. "It put extraordinary demands on us in terms of production when a story must happen on a planet or off the Enterprise," says Taylor. "We needed to have a substantial story on the Enterprise, which would take the pressure off of those sets and be as interesting as what was going on in that planet. So we thought 'Well, you know, we never used that story about Troi' and Ron was able to make that very believable in a way that it hadn't been before. I thought it was really strong, although we have taken some criticism from people who said 'how could you promote her over Data and Geordi?' But it would not have been a very interesting story to see Geordi or Data getting their rank. The obstacles she had to overcome were formidable and where you get interesting drama is out of conflict."

"I thought that was a neat idea and was a good move for the character," says Ron Moore of Troi's promotion. "The whole notion was something I wanted to do ever since I read Jeri Taylor's novel-

ization of 'Unification,' where there is a line about Troi reflecting on her experiences in the episode 'Disaster' where she got command temporarily. Jeri had a line in there about tasting blood and wanting to again, and that stuck with me. I thought that was an interesting direction to take Troi."

As for the episode as a whole, Moore notes, "I have mixed feelings about it. As a writer, I never figured out what it was about. I didn't know what I was trying to say with the episode. It was probably the most difficult writing experience I had on the show because I was very frustrated. It was a bad time in the season. I was tired and I was not having fun, and I think it showed in the writing. When I got this episode, I felt like I didn't have anything to say. What I enjoyed writing was Data as Mr. Wizard on the planet of people who aren't very smart. That was kind of funny. I got a kick of Data being the guy in the back of the class raising his hand, inventing quantum mechanics with stone knives and bear skins."

Adds Brannon Braga, "It was great to see an episode as fundamental as Data being forced to confront his inner nature. The cool factor was also very high. Seeing Data impaled by a metal rod was just great. I enjoyed the episode. A couple of the performances of townsfolk were a little groggy for my taste, but Data as Frankenstein — what a neat idea. I thought, all in all, it was a very nice job. In fact, I thought it was probably one of the best ones of this season."

Offers director Winrich Kolbe, "It was interesting because I had done 'Pen Pals,' a show that didn't quite find the right direction. Data seems to have a predilection for little girls, not in a bad way. Here we wind up again with a little girl. There seems to be something about Data that gives writers the idea for the relationship. He has a vulnerability or an innocence, especially at the beginning. It's Brent at his best. I liked the episode. We got some good actors and it was almost like a period piece. It was like going back to the Renaissance."

Episode #169
"Masks"
Original Airdate: **2/21/94**
Written by **Joe Menosky**
Directed by **Robert Wiemer**

The Enterprise encounters an alien probe which hooks into Data, endowing him with varying personalities from among its civilization while it begins transforming the Enterprise into an ancient city. Only by assuming the persona of one of the mythological characters in the alien lore, can Picard prevent the total reconfiguration of the Enterprise.

*****

Actor Brent Spiner, who had just completed shooting "Thine Own Self", was admittedly unhappy to be given such little prep time to prepare

for "Masks," an episode which required that he portray a number of personas who have taken over his android body.

"I had some good stuff seventh season," says Spiner. "I just wish they had been scheduled differently. I got the script for 'Masks' on the night before we shot it and I was finishing 'Thine Own Self' the midnight before, so I didn't have the time to even absorb the script and digest it and figure out who these people were that I was playing. You could look at it as an opportunity and I would.... under normal circumstances.

"I think I said to Jeri at the time, 'Give me six months and I think I could give all the characters their due, but as it was, I didn't know who these people were and so I was doing instant acting and just coming up with whatever I was coming up with because we had to put it on film.'"

"Brent was very nervous about doing all of those parts," confirms Taylor. "He said Dustin Hoffman had a year to figure out how to do Tootsie and portray a woman. I said 'You don't have to portray a woman, just portray a leader.' He ended up carving up four unique, distinct personalities which are very, very tough on an actor, especially given the time constraints."

"I remember seeing the initial story and saying, 'Jesus, what is this?'" recalls Ron Moore of the original treatment by overseas *Trek* scribe Menosky. "It was pretty out there and then the script came in and we all sort of scratched our heads and looked at each

other and wondered what he's smoking out there in the Alps? But when we started to examine it and get into it a little more, we saw what he was doing. He has some real interesting ideas and he approaches things from a fresh angle. It was a fascinating episode. It was just full of wild concepts and from that angle alone it was worth doing. Sometimes you have to take those risks and really go out someplace and do something bizarre."

"Joe is one of those writers who has a unique vision that no one else understands," says Brannon Braga. "Shows need to be nurtured by him and it's very tough to come in on one of his scripts and start rewriting it. He needed to be here and it's unfortunate that it suffered as a result. The first draft had some very confusing elements that needed work. On the whole, it was a very good script, but the last act was unsatisfying and I feel that was because it needed to be simplified, but Joe wasn't here to do it and the staff struggled a little bit. Joe's one of those writers who has a vision and it's tough to second guess it. The best thing about the show is watching the Enterprise being mutated into this weird ancient civilization. The art direction, effects and the opticals were among our best."

Episode #170
"Eye of the Beholder"
Original Airdate: **2/28/94**
Teleplay by **Rene Echevarria**
Story by **Brannon Braga**
Directed by **Cliff Bole**
Guest Starring:
Mark Rolston (Walter Pierce),
Nancy Harewood (Lt. Nara),
Tim Lounibos (Lt. Kwan),
Johanna McCloy (Calloway)

During an investigation into an officer's suicide, Troi is overwhelmed with psychic images dating back to the ship's construction eight years prior. Before you can say "psychic residual trace, hyperkeritosis in the plasma injectors," Troi finds herself in a tempestuous affair with Worf, jealously eyeing his interest in a younger Ensign, in what turns out to be a dream. Ultimately, Troi's visions hold the key to the man who was responsible for the murder.

*****

"The story was actually at one point rejected," says Brannon Braga. "We had heavy scrutiny coming on every episode that we tried to get passed, but there came a point where we hit a real rough dry spot in the season where we had to have stories. We resurrected this because we thought it was worthwhile and the producers took a second look with a different viewpoint and ended up saying go ahead and give it a try."

• • • •

Says Jeri Taylor, "Brannon had this story idea around for a while. It wasn't a murder mystery but had to deal with a haunted room on the Enterprise and it sort of evolved into a murder mystery. By this point of the season, we were getting down to the very tough crunch in which Ron

and Brannon were writing the final episode and I was running out of writers. Brannon, of course, wanted to do his own teleplay but was already on to the final episode, so Rene took it over and did a very nice job with it.

"It was confusing," she adds. "We were hindered by our production restraints. You can do a story in which someone has a hallucination or a dream and make that real clear to the audience if you do it in a location that you never visit at any time except when that hallucination begins or ends. We didn't have that luxury. We had one set, so unfortunately it was utterly perplexing as to exactly when did the hallucination start. I can only say I realize that and I'm sorry for it. I hope that the episode had enough shear mystery to draw one along. I think it did. You never knew quite what was going on there. And, of course, this was where we reprised the second part of our Worf/Troi romance. But, again, it wasn't real. There was nothing substantive in it in either time frame."

Adds Braga, "The Worf/Troi element was not there in my original story and didn't come about until the break session in the same way that it evolved in 'Parallels.' Personally, I found the Worf/Troi angle the least satis-

fying part of the show in the end, because it was a shaggy dog story. It's a unique couple. They have had a romantic interlude in an alternate reality, in a hallucination and, in the final episode, in an alternate time line. They have yet to get together. It's bizarre, really, and in that regard I found it sort of unsatisfying because after 'Parallels,' I think audience expectations were so high, people were eager to see them get together and when it ended and it was a hallucination, it was disappointing. On the whole, I thought it was a good mystery. It was fun to watch. I thought Rene did a nice job with the Data scene where Data is talking about having thought about killing himself. That was rather surprising. Perhaps that's what the episode should have been about dramatically, instead of a shaggy dog romance."

"The idea that what Troi experiences happens in the blink of an eye came about in the break session, and we were all very concerned about whether that was going to work," Braga continues. "In the end, it was a little confusing. Rene came up with an idea that it was really happening and in the end she starts to see through someone's eyes on the ship and realizes she's seeing through the killer's eyes. It's kind of *The Eyes of Laura*

Mars routine. The finale was going to be Troi being stalked from her own point of view."

"I think it is one of our better murder mysteries," says Ron Moore. "I think it sustains the illusion that you are really on the Enterprise for quite some time until you finally start to get wise and realize something is up. "

Episode #171
"Genesis"
Original Airdate: 3/21/94
Written by **Brannon Braga**
Directed by **Gates McFadden**
Guest Starring:
Patti Yasutake (Ogawa),
Dwight Schultz (Barclay)

When Barclay gets the flu, Dr. Crusher inadvertently triggers a genetic virus in an attempt to cure him, which begins to slowly transform the crew into primitive creatures by altering their genetic make-up. Riker is ultimately turned into an ape Barclay into an arachnid, and Troi into an amphibian-like creature.

Returning to the ship, Picard and Data must engineer a cure for the virus before Picard is affected and the Enterprise becomes a "starship of the apes."

*****

In Braga's original draft, Data's anti-virus injection was going to turn the entire crew into Barclay. "They discover that the mutated T-cell which came from Barclay isn't just turning people into proto-creatures, but is then going to end up turning everyone into Barclay and restructuring the genetic sequences, which I thought would have been a lot of fun. Mike Piller thought it was one step too far and in the end, when I sat down to write it, I felt he was probably right."

"I think 'Genesis' is classic *Star Trek*," enthuses Ron Moore. "It is right in the spirit of the original series to have everybody in the ship start to become animals. It is very high concept *Trek* and it could have only been written by Brannon."

"Genesis" marked actress Gates McFadden's directorial debut. "It was very unlike normal *Star Trek*," she observes. "It was very spooky and it starts off with a lot of comedy and all of a sudden it turns out very dark. Many of my favorite shots were cut out and they were only seen in the directors cut. When the shuttle craft first comes back, I had a fabulous thing where I had choreographed some steadi-cam shots and everything was incredibly dark. They cut all that out and put in this part that was at the very tail end that I never intended to use, that showed whole shuttle bay and it was very well lit. We also didn't see the excrement of the proto-creatures. There

was a line where Picard says 'What's that smell?' and Data says the technical term for excrement. It was very funny, there were piles of shit all over the floor."

"Gates is very well versed in dance and movement, so she really coached the actors in how to move with animal-like movements rather than Starfleet-like people in a mask," adds Jeri Taylor. "The opportunity to direct had been given to a number of other male actors on the show and the feeling was that she deserved the chance. She studied very hard. She worked as an observer for days on other episodes and came to production meetings and really plunged herself into it. It was a very committed endeavor on her part."

Braga notes the origin of the story idea, reflecting his desire to "do something with latent genes in altered states, but I knew that I wanted to do something that was even more believable and wild, hence all of the creatures that evolved along the evolutionary chain. People liked the idea and it was fun to write." In the case of one of Braga's creations, Lt. Barclay as an arachnid, the choice seemed natural. "I just thought it would be fun to make Barclay a spider because I can't imagine anything more awful to become. It just seemed natural since he's a kind of nervous and wiry guy, that maybe he would have had more arachnid ancestors than the other ones, but who knows why we are the way we are today? Maybe latent genetic structures help shape the personalities we have."

Some of the episode's content, which is one of the series' more violent episodes, almost seems like *Alien*-lite, particularly when Worf spews an acid-like substance on to Dr. Crusher. "It was violent and it was in a way more shocking because it's a beloved character," says Braga. "It's weird to see our beloved Beverly screaming in agony and writhing on the floor. This may sound lofty, but I think the difference is that our show has higher aims than say a show with no moral or thematic underpinnings. Our show strives to give more depth — whether it's thematic or ethical issues — so in that way it differs from a show that's just T&A and violence. I think we can get away with a little more and the violence we convey has more impact. You don't see people shot to pieces every week on our show, and yet our show was rated one of the fifth most violent shows on the air by some independent survey company. I don't know why. In the case of

'Genesis', in some strange way venom spewing was okay because it was almost like watching a nature show. If it had been, say, Worf grabbing a vile of acid and throwing it in Beverly's face, I bet you that wouldn't have been acceptable. When it's an act of nature vs. an act of intellectual violence, that's an important distinction."

Charged with metamorphosizing the crew of the Enterprise into proto-creatures was the show's make-up supervisor, Michael Westmore. "Most of our time was spent with Michael Westmore," says Jeri Taylor. "We knew that this episode would rise or fall on the basis of the make up. Our fear was that if it were hokey and over the top, then it would seem just buffoonish and Michael did his usual superb job of making things seem a natural outgrowth of the people. You bought it all. Marina's willingness to look as bizarre as she did in this and to go completely away from glamour to this gilled, gasping creature was remarkably bold for an actor."

Critiques Ron Moore, "Just watching Dwight Schultz do his impersonation of a spider running through the ops lounge was worth the price of admission, and watching Riker getting progressively stupider was just delightful stuff."

Episode #172
"Journey's End"
Original Airdate: **3/28/94**
Written by **Ronald D. Moore**
Directed by **Corey Allen**
Guest Starring:
Wil Wheaton (Wesley Crusher), Tom Jackson (Lakanta), Natalija Nogulich (Admiral Necheyev), Ned Romero (Anthwara), George Aguilar (Wakasa), Richard Poe (Gul Evek), Eric Menyuk (Traveller), Doug Wert (Jack Crusher)

Wesley Crusher returns to the Enterprise struggling with whether or not to remain in Starfleet, when Admiral Necheyev orders Picard into the newly created dimilitarized zone to lead the evacuation of a tribe of Native American Indians from Cardassian territory. When they refuse to vacate the planet, Wesley joins with them to prevent them from being forcibly moved. Later, one of the Native Americans, who has brought about Wesley's spiritual awakening, is revealed as the Traveller, who then helps the young ensign transcend this plane of existence to join with him in exploring the cosmos.

*****

"We started out by saying we were doing two things at once," says Michael Piller. "My son had come in and pitched with his friend an episode about a Native American Indian colony and the problems of them trying to move out of the neutral zone. He had tied it to Riker and the story of his father dying. I didn't want to do another story of a family member dying. At the same time, Ron and Jeri were struggling with the Wesley story and Ron had very much wanted to tie the Wesley story into the Maquis introduction, but it was never a very comfortable marriage. As an episode, I was quite pleased with it and it turned out better in a number of ways than I expected it might. The Wesley story was something I was less than satisfied with but I think it could have worked. The resolution didn't seem to come out of the story. It seemed to have come from the need to resolve it and that always bothers me when that occurs."

Ron Moore had begun to develop a very unique arc for the character of Wesley Crusher in fifth season's "The First Duty," in which he took the interesting and unexpected approach of including Wesley in a conspiracy to hide the fact that he and several fellow cadets were responsible for the death of a peer at Starfleet Academy.

"I thought 'First Duty' was a genuine turn for the character of Wesley and I thought it really moved him to a different place and level. I wanted to keep going with that," says Ron Moore. "I also identified with him more strongly in that episode than in a lot of the shows. It's a very personal show for me because I went through a lot of the same things. I had a lot of the same background. My father was a military officer, I grew up with that. I thought I wanted that for myself, but there were all of these other little things in my life as far as writing and the arts that I was doing. I had initially wanted Wesley to just leave the Academy and say he was going to work at the Daystrom Institute or go off and discover himself or something like that. That ran into resistance and the story went up and down all season long. I finally got Michael onboard who said, `If he is going to leave the Academy, I think Wesley has to go on to something greater instead of just being another scientist.' He felt, as one of our heroes, he should go on to something greater and he said, if you bring back the Traveller than you have him take Wesley to some cosmic journey, that I can accept."

Interestingly, Moore had initially toyed with making the Traveller Boothby, the Starfleet Academy groundskeeper Picard first talked about in second season's "Samaritan Snare." The idea was rejected by Michael Piller. However one idea that did prove important in the episode was the inclusion of the Maquis, the first *Star Trek* installment to set up the backstory for the new *Voyager* series.

"We felt that this would provide a background for *Voyager* by setting up this Native American culture who had left earth 200 years ago to preserve a way of life and so that in *Voyager* we have our character, Chakotay, who comes from that background with one foot in the 21st century and one in an earlier era," says Jeri Taylor. "We realized in producing 'Journey's End' that this may be fraught with peril. Native Americans have become a highly politicized voice who are articulate and emphatic and demanding in the way that they have been depicted in the past and the way they want to be depicted now. We hired a Native American as a consultant to help us avoid some of these pitfalls, but what we learned was that there seems to be very little agreement, even among Native American nations. You are probably going to offend somebody at some point no matter what you do. We intended to treat the Native American culture with the utmost respect and show the value of some of their metaphysical ways of approaching life, that it is positive and valuable but even in the depiction of that, we ran into trouble with some groups who don't want that depicted at all."

"It was an added element," says Ron Moore of the inclusion of the Maquis and the Native American aspect of the script. "We had talked about setting up the Maquis in that episode first, and then using the Native American culture came along the same way. I was just so desperate to do the story that any A story they were going to let me do, I grabbed onto because I wanted to do a Wesley show. I said, 'Oh yeah, the Maquis, okay great, oh yeah the American Indians, great. Whatever you are going to let me do with this, I will marry an A story to it.' It was fun to do and it was a very serpentine process to get to the final episode as far as the Indian culture that was there. We started off and we said, 'Okay, we will do the Hopi Indians, make them all Hopi Indians.' Then we found out that might cause certain problems. Maybe the Hopis don't want to be represented on television, they get very sensitive about that. So we decided should we go with another tribe or should we just try to make it a mythical tribe or should we just not say who they are? This is a sensitive issue for a lot of people and

these people have the right to be sensitive considering their history. They're understandably careful about what they like said about them and who says what. So there was a lot of internal back and forth about what would be best. We knew we were not going to be able to please everybody, but it was done with the best of intentions and I hope it was well received."

Says Jeri Taylor of sending Wesley on his cosmic journey with the Traveller, "I'm delighted when we ruffle the audience. I believe that good drama makes people feel something. It should not make them feel content and passive and comfortable. It should shake them up and make them feel stronger kinds of emotions. If people are moved to write because they don't like something, that to me is an indication that we've done our job. This story was lying around a long time. It was a story that Ron Moore has wanted to tell for two or three years because it's a story that is very close to him. He saw parallels with Wesley making the decision to leave Starfleet. Ron too was a young man who lived up to everybody's expectations and was headed for the career that people expected him to be headed for and he ultimately changed his mind and said I want to do what I

want to do rather than what I'm expected to do and took the perilous step of deciding to become a writer. As a parent, I can only sympathize with what his parents must have gone through at that point. Wesley too was sort of geared toward going to Starfleet from 'Farpoint' on. He was Gene Roddenberry's alter ego and was following his father, and his surrogate father's footsteps, and he was on the track that everybody expected and it seemed like an important statement for today's young people to take stock of themselves, to look into their hearts and to make the choices which they feel are right for them — even if it means flying in the face of everybody else's wishes."

"The story was a battle between Ron, myself, Michael and Rick with everybody having different positions at different points, with Michael particularly feeling that to have Wesley leave Starfleet was in a sense a slap in Gene Roddenberry's face and that it would be very unsatisfying and disappointing to the audience to see him turn his back on everything that he was working for. Ron and I were the champions of wanting to give him the ability to determine his own fate. Rick was on different sides at different points. Ultimately, it was Michael's idea to turn his leaving Starfleet into a positive and unexpected thing and have him go off with the Traveller to begin a study of something that we can't even articulate because we don't know what it means. It's another plane of existence. Wesley was intended for something even greater than Starfleet, so he's going to go onto something more positive, more elevated rather than simply turning his back on something that is very positive and going off to be a shoe salesman."

Episode #173
"Firstborn"
Original Airdate: **4/25/94**
Teleplay by **Rene Echevarria**
Story by **Brian Kalbfeld**
Directed by **Jonathan West**
Guest Starring:

Brian Bonsall (Alexander), Barbara March (Lursa), Gwynith Walsh (B'Etor), Joel Swetow (Yog), Colin Mitchell (Gorta), Rickey D'Shon Collins (Eric), John Shull (Molor), James Sloyan (K'Mtar), Armin Shimerman (Quark)

An adult Alexander comes back in time as K'Mtar, to try and prevent Worf's death. After an assassination attempt is make, apparently on Worf's life, at a Klingon celebration, the Enterprise begins an investigation which leads to Lursa and B'Etor, who claim to have been uninvolved with the murder attempt. It is only when K'Mtar attempts to kill Alexander that Worf learns the truth from his son.

*****

"This story came to us as a pitch from a freelance writer which had nothing to do Alexander," says Jeri Taylor. "It had to do with the Romulans and a ship from the future which turned out not even to be a ship from the future, but a ploy by the Romulans. We had bought that story and he wrote it, but it just seemed a little ordinary so we started messing around with it during one of our brainstorming sessions and then we just hit on the idea that Alexander comes back from the future to kill his young self. That seemed wonderful but for a long time that's all we had. We didn't know why he did this. Michael had thought that it had the scope, perhaps at one point, to be a two parter. We tried that. It didn't seem there was enough to make it a two parter. We finally decided to make it one episode and hammered it out I think it's really one of the most original sci-fi premises."

Says Michael Piller, "There was a big fight all year long about an episode that they desperately wanted to do that I would not let them do about Alexander getting kidnapped and coming back as a 25-year-old. He's totally lost his youth and is dealing with the consequences of this and I just thought it was a nasty thing that we were basically taking the kid's entire childhood away. I just wouldn't go for it. However, I fell in love with the idea of 'First Born' in which we address the psychological implications of a man who feels a failure, who comes back to his own youth to destroy himself at a young age, in order to avoid the pain that he has caused and suffered. There is a tremendous science-fiction premise in that. And if you have been in on any of my therapy, you know that I've dealt with this on a number of different levels."

Interestingly, it had originally been planned that K'ehlyr, Worf's Klingon mate played by Suzi Plakson, would return as well. "It was originally intended that there would be a third mystery character, who was K'ehlyr coming back to intervene between this man's quest to kill himself as a child and that only changed because the actor was not interested in coming back. I know Rick breathed a sigh of relief because he did not like the idea in the first place. But for better or worse, that might have helped the episode."

The episode was written by Rene Echevarria who assumed the mantle of Klingon scribe from Ron Moore, who had helped craft some of the best of the many Klingon episodes. "I was out of the Klingons, but Rene has a good feel for them," says Ron Moore. "He brings a different cultural flavor to the Klingons than what I did. The stuff he did sixth season in 'Birthright' and then what he did with them here is very interesting. Worf and Alexander celebrate at a Klingon outpost and they have this sort of mock opera singing, heroic fights and re-enactments of things in the streets and banners and this was a whole different cultural flavor to these guys that I hadn't thought of. My take on the Klingons was sort of more Shakespearean with the House of Mogh and that kind of stuff, and the rise and fall of political players. Rene brings in a much different element which I think serves them well."

Casting James Sloyan as Alexander's adult self was fraught with its own difficulties, since Sloyan had recently shot a *Deep Space Nine* playing Dr. Pol, Odo's Bajoran caretaker, in "The Alternate."

"This was the second time in which we found ourselves with the perfect actor," recalls Jeri Taylor. "When he came in, he just nailed it and we were then told we couldn't use him because he had been on *Deep Space Nine* and Michael and Rick were afraid that he'd be recognizable. I

looked at the *Deep Space Nine* footage and said 'No, no, no. He was a Bajoran, now he's going to be a Klingon. You'd never recognize anybody in Klingon make up.' They felt that his voice would be recognizable and so we kept looking and looking. We must have read 35 to 40 people and there was just no one like James Sloyan. I went back to them and asked them to reconsider. I said, 'This can be a really strong episode or this can be a so-so episode. It will depend on whoever plays that part,' and they relented. We got James Sloyan and I will defy anybody to know the two roles were played by the same person."

Comments Michael Dorn, who Taylor now describes as the "Mr. Mom" of Klingons, "We don't really know what happens now. Just that the future is uncertain. It's just like real life, but Worf is still a terrible father. He hasn't got a clue."

Episode #174
"Bloodlines"
Original Airdate: 5/2/94
Written by **Nicholas Sagan**
Directed by **Les Landau**

DaiMon Bok (from first season's "The Battle") returns to get revenge against Picard for the death of his son, by genetically engineering Jason Vigo to appear to be Picard's

illegitimate child. By creating a son for Picard and convincing him of his veracity, Bok then plans to kill Vigo and finally get his long simmering vengeance against the captain. It is only when the deception is revealed by Beverly Crusher

• • • •

and Bok's fellow Ferengi learn that there is no profit in vengeance, that Bok is once again stopped before he can cause any further harm.

*****

"This episode came about because I was on the set of 'Masks' and I was standing with Brent and Patrick and said are there any aspects of your character we haven't explored?'" recalls Jeri Taylor of the genesis of DaiMon Bok's return. "Patrick said, 'It's always fascinated me that there is this creature running around the universe even now who despises me,' and that seemed interesting. I talked to Michael about it and Michael was very open to the idea. Nick Sagan came up with the idea of this son who was cloned so that Bok could kill Picard's son as Picard had killed his own. It wasn't until we were really into it that we realized that this was, in a sense, ground that we had covered in a funny way not just with `Suddenly Human' but with Wesley since Picard was a surrogate father to him. Fortunately, Patrick gives probably the most vulnerable performance of his career. He opened himself to this young man in a way that I have not seen him do. He was absolutely raw and open and hurting. I think by the power of his performance he

brings this to another level of emotional intensity that takes it away from any of those other episodes."

Not everyone was as interested in whatever happened to DaiMon Bok, including some of the show's writers. "I wondered if the world knew or cared if DaiMon Bok came back again," laughs Ron Moore. "I wasn't a big fan of that or 'The Battle' and I didn't see the point of repeating 'Suddenly Human' where we really nailed an interesting arc with Picard having a sort of father/son relationship."

Nick Sagan, who was saddled with the premise, jumped at a chance to once again pen a *Next Generation* episode, but was admittedly underenthused with the story premise he had been charged with bringing to life.

"Jeri said we are trying to do a bottle show because of budget and she told me that she had talked to Patrick Stewart who wanted to see the return of DaiMon Bok from 'The Battle.' I remembered him and I liked the kind of twisted, nasty villain he was and remembered thinking it was one of the few cool episodes first season. She said Patrick was interested in doing something with that character coming back seeking revenge, and to come up with something on that. I said sure and tried to

think what it was that he would do. I figured Bok would try and get revenge against Picard's son and who would that be? Is Picard's son the ship? No, Kirk's son is the Enterprise. I decided to make it a genetically engineered pseudo son. Originally, it was a much darker episode.

Originally called "Fugue," the idea was that Bok had genetically engineered this kid from birth and advanced his growth and had been giving him memories of Picard abandoning him on the Stargazer. Then Bok was using one of the mind balls to give Picard these vague flashes of false memories, making him think that it was possible he had this sort of fugue-like experience where he basically abandoned his son on the Stargazer and blocked it out of his mind.

Adds Sagan, "I don't know if it would have ever worked or not, but it was kind of a really interesting, dark aspect and it gave you a sense of abandonment and trying to sort of recapture this sort of sense of a son that he never had. Then it turns out that it's not that at all."

At the time, Sagan didn't realize one of the reasons the producers rejected his early story concept was that writers Braga and Moore had used Picard being the last of his family line as an important subplot in their script for the first *Star Trek* feature film, and wished to avoid treading on that ground in the episode.

Episode #175
"Emergence"
Original Airdate: 5/9/94
Written by **Brannon Braga & Joe Menosky**
Directed by **Cliff Bole**
Guest Starring:
Thomas Kopache (Engineer), David Huddleston (Conductor), Arlee Reed (Hayseed), Vinny Argiro (Dixon Hill)

A mysterious holodeck malfunction which sends a steam locomotive through Data's performance of *The Tempest*, leads the crew to investigate puzzling anomalies on the holodeck which are creating a series of bizarre images after taking control of the ship. The passengers aboard the locomotive, the Orient Express, are on their way to "New Veriform City," which we later learn is a sector of space where the Enterprise helps give birth to a new alien lifeform.

*****

"I felt if we were going to do another holodeck show, we should do one like we've never seen before," says Braga. "It's a bizarre amalgam of all the holodeck shows we've ever seen. I had in my mind this image of Dixon Hill crossed with King Arthur's Court crossed with the Old West crossed with Modern Day New York - all thrown together and our people trapped in this adventure. I thought that would be neat and ended up coming up with the concept of the ship developing a psyche. These subconscious elements of that psyche would manifest themselves on the Holodeck and we have to go in and interpret the symbiology and communicate to the ship through the adventures that it's portraying."

Adds Ron Moore, "I think that holodeck stuff is a riot. The re-creation of the Orient Express alone is worth the price of admission.

Episode #176
"Preemptive Strike"
Original Airdate: 5/16/94
Teleplay by **Rene Echevarria**
Story by **Naren Shankar**
Directed by **Patrick Stewart**
Guest Starring:
Michelle Forbes (Ro Laren), John Franklyn - Robbins (Macias), Natalija Nogulich (Admiral Nechayev), William Thomas, Jr. (Santos), Shannon Cochran (Kalita), Richard Poe (Gul Evek)

Ensign Ro Laren returns and is recruited by Starfleet and Captain Picard to infiltrate the Maquis, a rebel band of Federation citizens within the demilitarized zone between the Federation and Cardassian territory. Her objective is to prevent a secret attack on a Cardassian installation. During her time undercover, Ro finds herself becoming attached to those among the Maquis resistance, ultimately deciding — however reluctantly — to

betray Picard and join with them to protect their home against the Cardassians.

*****

"We were in a real bind for a story and we were racking our brains to come up with things," says Naren Shankar. "Ron and I were kicking around some ideas, we talked about doing a *Next Generation/DS9* crossover. We started to put one together, but it didn't quite work. It was about someone seeking asylum on DS9. We were talking about this and we thought wouldn't it be funny if that person seeking asylum was Ensign Ro. Michael thought that was interesting, so we started going on about getting Ensign Ro into the story, testing her loyalties, having her relationship with Picard go somewhere and seeing some resolution to that character."

Notes Jeri Taylor of recruiting Michelle Forbes back to the *Trek* fold, "We contacted Michelle's people and the word came back to me that it was possible she would do it, but it would depend on a phone conversation I would have with her in telling her about this story to see if it was a story she wanted to do. Well, this was the next to the last episode and we didn't have a story. We had days before we had to write a script. We couldn't take the time to

develop a story if we didn't know that she was going to be doing it. So I got on the phone with her and did a tap dance. I was concocting things out of thin air. Ro does this and she does that and this is an intense story of a woman's personal, moral dilemma. It sounded very intense and emotional and apparently it worked because within minutes after I had gotten off the phone with her, the word came back that she had called and would do the episode. Then we had to write the story and make it something like what I had spun out.

"I think it's a great coup to get her," Taylor continues. "She's an outstanding actress and it's a character that everybody hated to see go. She does a wonderful job in it."

"Preemptive Strike" was originally titled "The Good Fight." Like "Journey's End," the episode would pave the way for *Voyager* by reinforcing the concept of the Maquis. "The Maquis really existed," says Jeri Taylor. "That was the name of the French resistance fighters in World War II. My husband ironically wrote a teleplay about the real Maquis about thirty years or so ago. They call themselves freedom fighters, the Federation calls them outlaws. They are the people who have taken up arms to defend themselves against Cardassian strikes in the newly created Cardassian de-militarized zone. It's a situation not unlike that of the west bank in Israel where people have been displaced and have to move from homes they've had for a while because of diplomatic deci-

sions. Lines are drawn in space and people get upset by that. And the people who are in that zone have very volatile emotions and beliefs and start throwing rocks at each other. The Cardassians are being supplied secretly by their government because they have a vested interest in keeping the region unstable and trying to drive out the Federation citizens. The citizens take matters into their own hands and start doing more than defending themselves by making preemptive strikes. It's a situation that will quickly get out of hand. Starfleet fears them, so they must control it. These are renegades. They are outlaws. They must be stopped. The Maquis, of course, are equally convinced that the Federation has let them down. That they have the right to defend themselves and their families. They have no intention of stopping."

Episodes #177 & 178
"All Good Things"
Original Airdate: 5/23/94
Written by **Ronald D. Moore and Brannon Braga**
Directed by **Winrich Kolbe**
Guest Starring:
John DeLancie (Q), Denise Crosby (Tasha Yar)

Seven years of starship voyages come to an end as Picard confronts a juxtaposition of time periods in an attempt to solve a puzzling

galactic mystery which Q threatens will lead to the destruction of humanity. Propelled between three time-lines — the past, present and future — Picard joins with the crew of the Enterprise in each time period to prevent mankind's annihilation.

*****

Says finale co-writer Ron Moore, "The toughest thing was getting approval on the story because everyone wanted the story to be really, really special. There was a good week where we kept trying to get the story approved. Time was running out and it was just really frustrating. It was made more difficult by the fact that the final episode, ironically, was going to go into prep before the second to last episode, so there was even less time than there normally would be for the season finale which drove everybody crazy; the director, set designers, everybody on the whole production. The staff really had to go for it on this one."

Next to Richard Kimble finally capturing the One-Armed Man in the classic *Fugitive* series, it would be hard to find an episode of television that was more eagerly anticipated than the finale of *Star Trek: The Next Generation.*

In the show's projected alternative future, the crew is reunited on Picard's farm and Dr. Crusher now commands a medical ship, having been married to and divorced from Captain Picard. "I thought maybe I should have his fish in my ready room, skewered," laughs Gates McFadden of the unexpected twist on the Crusher/Picard relationship. "At the very least, I could have his Shakespeare text ripped in half on my desk."

"We knew since the beginning of the season that that episode was coming at us and would have to be done, and it was intimidating," recalls Jeri Taylor. "Any final episode of a series is unique and important and for a series

like *Star Trek*, which has cut such a niche in the American consciousness, the expectations are really very high.

"Brannon originally came up with the notion of time slipping, which he pitched as an episode idea," adds Taylor. "Michael seized on the idea as having the scope and epic qualities that a final episode should have. When we started breaking the story, we were really flying by the seat of our pants. It seems that some of our best work gets done under pressure, because the adrenaline starts running and we just started brainstorming."

"Michael Piller had some ideas we talked about early on," recalls Ronald D. Moore, who co-wrote the finale with Brannon Braga. "I had originally mentioned that Q should be in the final episode in a different context and Michael liked that idea and hung onto it. He said, `I think you should have Q and I think it should focus on Picard and I think it should have some time travel elements in it,' and then it was just a matter of trying to bring those ideas together."

Says Braga, "Once we had the initial concept of Q's involvement and time shifting, which I had suggested earlier in the season, it became a great struggle again for us because there was great scruti-

ny by everybody since it was the last episode. It just took a lot of work. The main problem is we didn't have a lot of time left to do it, so we were re-writing stories in one day and that was kind of tough."

Initially, the storyline which involves Picard time-shifting between the Enterprise's first mission to Farpoint, the present and the far future, in which many of the crew have become estranged, originally was going to include a fourth time period, the Borg attack in "Best of Both Worlds."

"There were going be two paths we were going to play out including part of the plotline in 'Best of Both Worlds' in which Hugh is aboard to save Picard. It would have been great to see that episode start to play out differently, but they felt it was just too much story and we'd better have only three time periods."

Even with the deletion of the Borg story arc, "All Good Things" was still an immensely complicated show both from the perspective of story and production logistics.

"We had to make the three time periods distinct from each other so the audience wouldn't get lost," says Moore.

Adds Taylor of *The Christmas Carol*-like awakening Picard undergoes, "We wanted to tell a story in which we realized that all the parts of a person's life contribute to making them what they are. Their past informs the present, the present informs the future and determines what they will be. That was the underlying kind of thematic material that we addressed in the context of an epic action/adventure which was still laden with a rich character story that we thought would leave no one disappointed. I think that Ron and Brannon did their finest work on the show. It has scope, it has action, it has humor, it has mystery and it's all packed into two romping hours. It's the quintessential final episode."

"We knew we wanted it to be special," says Braga, "and the culmination of everything that makes *Star Trek* special. It's really a combination of two premises. Ron had a premise floating around for the final episode where Q comes back to put us on trial again and I had an idea about jumping through time. It actually began as an Alexander story. I had this idea where Alexander would experience a time slip and trade places with his future self 25 years in the future. The future self would have come back to the past and we would do a story that intercuts between the past and future. It was just a

Worf/Alexander story, but Michael Piller liked it so much he said, `If you combine this with the Q idea, I think we may have two more episodes.' And what eventually happened was it became a story about Picard time-slipping through the past, present and future and Q's involvement in that and the destruction of humanity. I'm just thrilled with the episode. I think it really is a culmination of so many elements of this show that make it memorable. There are Romulan threats, Klingon adventures, space battles and time travel in the way you've never seen it before. Structurally, it is the most ambitious episode we've ever done. Telling a story that takes place in three different time periods and trying to tell a unique story line in each with unique characters in each and showing how the characters change in each, yet having the stories, ultimately, all have to relate with each one was a tremendous challenge."

The challenge of dealing with such an ambitious premise led to several long, hard, break sessions." We broke and rebroke that show and ended up having very little time to write it and then very little time to rewrite it," says Braga. "The most anxious time was when we had to do a page one rewrite on the first draft in

one week, but somehow it was appropriate that this happened on the final episode."

"Ron and Brannon didn't start writing his two hour episode until nine days before the prep date," says Jeri Taylor of the initial production meeting where the various creative teams meet to discuss what needs to be created to bring a script to the screen. "Those poor production people were behind right from the get-go because, of course, they could not finish writing the two hours in that time. We had a production meeting on the first hour and then we had a production meeting on the second hour, and then Michael and Rick Berman felt that the story wasn't working in the second hour so we had to go back and re-break the entire story all over again. The production people were magnificent in terms of rolling with this really severe punch of being flexible, good natured and understanding. We were sort of all in this together and somehow we all pulled together and made it happen."

Among the biggest challenges from a production standpoint was recreating the look of the original two-hour premiere, "Encounter At Farpoint," one of the time periods recreated in the finale. "They began combing the prop department for some of the things we had seven years ago including, the reclining chairs on the bridge that we had. There are many things that had already been tossed out and we had no way of getting back, so we had to recreate the same feeling as the pilot."

In producing the episode, David Livingston and Merri Howard's production team were challenged by the fact that they were only given the first hour of the script while Moore and Braga rushed to complete work on the second hour.

"The courtroom set was a very complicated and time-consuming set originally in the pilot, but we simplified it and worked out some of the kinks that existed previously in terms of working off the crane," says Livingston of rebuilding the post-atomic court in which Q tried humanity. "I think [director] Rick Kolbe solved the problems quite cleverly and made it look very interesting. The different timelines; past, present and future, were tough because we had to come up with makeup and wardrobe that were appropriate to those periods and determine how much we wanted to recreate the original pilot or not. For instance, Michael Dorn's makeup has changed considerably over the years and one of the questions we asked was whether or not we wanted to

go back and recreate exactly what he had looked like in the past. We decided it wouldn't be appropriate because his facial structure has changed."

"It was fun to talk about the different visual elements that we wanted to change in the sets like the Enterprise and the wardrobe and the communicators to try and key to the audience that each individual

• • • •

time period had a unique and different look," he continues. "I think we were pretty successful in doing that."

Complicating production on the final episode was a last-minute rewrite mandated by executive producer Michael Piller. "The script was in continual rewrites and we had a major rewrite right before going into production," says Livingston. "It put all the pressure on the director and Kolbe is a director who does immaculate preparation, which he was not permitted to do because of the time constraints. He was always having to spend an extraordinary amount of time just keeping current with what was going on as well as contending with the schedule, which was an extraordinarily difficult schedule. But he is a man who exists with grace under pressure. He was a point man in Vietnam, so I guess after that nothing's gonna rattle him too much."

Which is not to say that the production schedule didn't bother him. While "All Good Things" was an emotional show, Kolbe emphasizes that it was a memorable experience production-wise.

"The show changed quite a bit from the original script to the final shooting script," Kolbe explains. "Unfortunately, for most of us it changed too late. I think out

of the 14 days of preparation I had, I sat around for nine days and the last five days were just a frantic struggle to get it all together. The show basically was rewritten. The general idea was there, but scenes were completely rewritten. The problem for me was that these scenes had to be tied together very carefully. There were transitions in there that were given in the script and I was expected to continue these transitions so that if Picard made a particular head move in the past, the moment we switched over that head move would pop up in the present or future. All of these things had to be choreographed."

Kolbe details that his approach is to prep from "the inside out." He reads the script so that he understands what the scenes are about, where they're coming from, where they're going, what are the objectives and what are the dramatic points. From there, he begins staging.

"I think every good director works that way," he muses. "Unfortunately, without a script that's kind of hard to do. When I finally got the script, I said to myself, 'Do I want to spend my time on the set trying to figure out how I'm going to shoot everything? Or do I start prepping from the outside and eliminate some of

the logistics, eliminate some of the staging; try to figure out what is happening in a scene and hope that I'm right? If I don't really understand what's going on, I've got Patrick, I've got Jonathan. I've got everybody else who's been doing this for years. They'll help me.' Well, it almost worked out that way. But, unfortunately, tensions were rather taut on that episode."

For one thing, he says, it was the last episode. Even though there was going to be a feature film, mortality was "rearing its ugly head," and the actors, he observed, were trying to reconcile themselves to the fact that the next job they would go to would probably be one they would have to read for.

"Even though they might say they're glad it's over, I'm sure they all have an ambiguous feeling," he offers. "That's what created the tension. Yes, we want it to end because we have done it and we're bored with it. On the other hand, it's security, it's safety, we don't have to sell shoes. Unfortunately, the movie was there and everybody, especially Patrick, was involved in the movie-making, the script conferences. There were all these problems and those problems took away from attention being given to this particular show. So the best laid plans of mice and men began to crumble rather early in the shooting and we had to struggle. There was a lot of tension. There was a lot of fun as well.

"It's a show that I would never want to do again and would love to do again," Kolbe smiles. "I think that's the feeling we all had. I'm very proud of what we did. It's a good looking show, we gave it a dignified ending, but, boy, what a pain in the ass it was to shoot."

The rewrites on the show were not lost on the cast, who were concerned by the changes being ordered by Piller.

"I got more involved in this than I have on any show on the *Next Generation* for two years," says Piller. "I actually went into the room with the guys and we rewrote the story because it wasn't working. This became controversial because for the first time in four years, Patrick Stewart called me up after seeing the first and later drafts and said, 'I'm terribly unhappy with the changes made in the script.' The problem with the first draft was that the guys were trying to bring as much character interplay into two hours as they possibly could, but there was no plot as far as I was concerned. They were on their way to something until Act 9

in a 10 Act structure. I knew in my gut that Act 9 had to be moved to Act 6. Instead of it being a romp with very schticky things that people loved, I wanted it to end with an adventure and a mystery."

Not everyone agreed. Brent Spiner was another of the actors disappointed by the rewrites on the finale, "The first draft that Ron and Brannon wrote was extraordinary," Spiner says. "I think it would have easily been thought of as the greatest *Star Trek* episode of all time. Michael came in and added a few thousand words of technobabble to it and took out some of the character scenes, which he is not keen on. There were moments when I read the first draft that my heart jumped into my throat because I was so excited. There were some wonderful moments between Picard, Geordi and Data. Nonetheless, it's still a very good episode."

One of the sequences which was lost in the rewrite involved Picard, Data and Geordi stealing the Enterprise so that they could travel to investigate the temporal anomaly in the future. "They go to the Starfleet Museum where the Enterprise is with a bunch of other ships and they get a guided tour," reveals Braga. "The tour guide doesn't even know who they are and they

have to commandeer the Enterprise to go on this crazy mission Picard wants to go on. Just as they're about to go, Admiral Riker comes in with a bunch of security people. They end up going anyway, of course, but to me that was a lot of fun. There was a lot of good character work that was lost. Did we need Geordi's visor to hold the key to the mystery? We've seen that about 25 times in the show. Do we really need his eyes to be getting younger? Would it have been better to have more character at the risk of meandering a little bit? Yes, I think so. But that's just my opinion. Michael Pillar's opinion is probably just as valid and I believe the show works either way. I'll tell you it was a lot more fun to write the scene of the crew stealing the Enterprise than it was to write tech about people getting younger and I believe what's more fun to write is more fun to watch."

Comments Ron Moore, "There were some things we just couldn't physically do which we talked about in production meetings. They promised they would do everything they could to recreate the Farpoint look on the Enterprise, but there are certain built-in limitations because some of those things just don't exist anymore. The way the viewscreen looked around the

SCI FI UNIVERSE ™

STAR TREK
THE NEXT GENERATION
FINAL SEASON

"I CAN'T BELIEVE IT'S OVER!"

$4.99 U.S./Canada • SEPTEMBER 1994

edges is a little different and the cost was just too much to make a whole new viewscreen. We re-carpeted the Enterprise, but who cares about that? Also, in the old days, the ops lounge and the sickbay were physically the same set which was just re-dressed. Now, they're different, so there were certain things we just said we'd shine. Do the best you can. Do the things that are going to be what your eye will visually go to, like the costumes, putting the gold ships back on the wall in ops."

One facet of the production that couldn't be changed was the fact that the cast had aged seven years since the pilot. "We talked about it," says Moore, "but there wasn't much we could do about that so we figured it was only seven years. It wasn't like asking the original series' actors trying to portray themselves in the 60's. I thought the audience would basically accept it and we were fortunate in that the Farpoint story happens to take Riker out of the picture because we weren't going to make Jonathan shave his beard and make him look younger. Fortunately, we found a clip of him to use with him on the monitor talking to Picard."

In addition to recreating the past, creating the future was equally daunting involving complex prosthetics for most of the cast. "The make up for the future was very difficult. It took time to put it on and we lost hours because of that," says Jeri Taylor. "Gates' skin, for instance, is very fragile and so the prosthetic that is added to her tends to kind of slip. Halfway through each day of shooting we had to completely redo her make-up from scratch."

David Livingston, the show's producer responsible for overseeing physical production on the series, comments, "The last show was an incredibly ambitious one in terms of scope and in terms of recapturing the pilot. I was directing an episode of *DS9* when [director Winrich] Kolbe started shooting, so I didn't have a lot of advice to offer based on my experience working on 'Farpoint,' but I did tell him the courtroom set was a very complicated and time-consuming set originally, in the pilot, and we simplified it and we worked out some of the kinks that existed before in terms of working off the crane. I think Rick Kolbe solved the problems quite cleverly and made it look very interesting."

For the writers, however, the fun was in postulating a future very different than what most viewers would expect. "We thought in what ways can they have become different?" muses Moore. "Some people should be estranged, we wanted somebody to be dead, we wanted Data to have become very human in the future. We wanted a lot of them to have left Starfleet. The notion that Beverly would be the captain of her own ship seemed like an outgrowth of some things we had started in the series, yet no one would really expect it. We really liked the idea that Geordi, the ultimate tech man, would become a novelist. It was fun coming up with their futureselves. Ultimately, it is an ambitious show and we took some major risks with the characters and that is good. I think it is a bold way to go out. But there was a lot of danger involved in trying to find the right balance of how much of a sci-fi mystery should it be? How much should it be of a valentine to the characters? How funny should it be? How much action? What will the Q part of it be? It was certainly the first time that we have dealt with a two-hour piece of the series where we didn't feel like we had to pad at some point. Usually at some point those two hours feel like we didn't have quite enough story to keep going. This one had so much story going on that trying to keep it all together within two hours was a bigger challenge."

As for the show's concluding moments in which Picard joins the senior staff at the poker table, Moore offers, "The poker game has become the signature of the series. It was a great idea that brought the crew together in a social situation. It's something we've always played through the years and it seems like them at their best, sitting around, off the bridge, just interacting with each other. Rick Berman's big note on the script was that he wanted the end of the series to have a sweet, nostalgic feel and he wanted everybody to walk away with a warm fuzzy feeling. That was his dictum to us."

Rick Kolbe remembers directing that particular poker game quite clearly. "That was a very simple climax to the show," he says. "Very well done. I think we shot that on the Friday before we finished. The next two days were basically the courtroom scenes between John DeLancie and Patrick Stewart. But the poker game was the last time that everybody from the regular crew was together. What you didn't see were the two hundred people around us, wanting to be there for this historic moment."

Inevitable comparisons cropped up in many cast and crew interviews between the two-hour finale, which boasted an epic scope, and the upcoming feature film, *Generations*. Says Moore, "I think it is inevitable that people will compare it. We just know that this could never have been the feature. It is such an inside show, you have to know the series a little bit and understand the characters and the relationships to appreciate it."

Adds Brannon Braga, "The final episode is too internal. It relies on knowledge of the show that is too much for a mainstream movie audience to have to know. It's structure is very radical. If the final episode were a movie, I'm convinced it would only play to an art house circuit. It makes *Slaughterhouse Five* look like *Sesame Street*."

Ultimately, most people would agree that "All Good Things" was a remarkable success in bringing to a close the logbooks of the Enterprise-D. With or without its moments of deeper character exploration, the show offered several insights of great relevance to today's world. "I think the episode is a true *Star Trek* adventure that works on a metaphorical level. It deals with the human condition and talks about all the issues that I think *Star Trek* really speaks to," enthuses Michael Piller. "There are some wonderful performances and Kolbe's direction was terrific. I think that the goal of the episode is not just to speculate about how families change, but also talk about how it takes a lifetime — or many lifetimes — for a man or mankind to create the problems that he has to deal with in this existence, and it also takes a lifetime for him to solve and address the issues and problems that he has created."

● ● ● ●

STAR TREK: GENERATIONS

Four days after the completion of photography on "All Good Things," the cast of *Star Trek: The Next Generation* began production on their first feature film, *Star Trek: Generations.*

Highlighted by the fact that it marked the coming together of Captains James T. Kirk and Jean Luc Picard, *Generations* was expected to be one of the biggest hits of Christmas '94. Unfortunately, it was greeted with mixed reviews and although it opened big (grossing $50 million in America within its first two weekends), the box office faded relatively quickly. Nonethless, it's generally believed that Paramount was satisifed with its performance and will readily finance a follow-up for release in 1996.

What follows are a series of articles looking at the making of that feature film, certainly the next logical step in the history of *Star Trek: The Next Generation.*

● ● ● ●

• • • •

Generations Genesis

To say that November 18, 1994 was a day being looked forward to with great anticipation by *Trek* fans is an understatement of dramatic proportion. From the moment the coming attractions trailer for *Star Trek: Generations* began unspooling in theaters playing Paramount's *Clear & Present Danger*, audiences had been primed for the release of the first of the *Trek* movies to feature the *Next Generation* crew brought to the big screen by many of the same creative team members who shepherded the weekly episodes to the small one.

"I found it fascinating and rewarding," says *Generations* producer Rick Berman of making the film, fulfilling many of the same functions as he did on the TV series. "I would say that my greatest accomplishment on the film was selecting terrific people, picking Ron and Brannon to write the script and working with them as well as selecting David Carson to direct. We had a great time and I think we have an absolutely drop dead, wonderful movie."

Enthuses co-screen-writer Brannon Braga, a veteran of *TNG* and a producer on the new *Star Trek: Voyager* series, "We knew it was big screen, cinemascope, and everything had to be bigger. We knew it had to have action, a villain, humor and less internal character scenes and less *Star Trek* lore. It had to be a film that someone who has never seen *Next Generation* in their life could sit down and enjoy."

Despite this fact, *Generations* boasts several familiar staples of the series, including the return of Lursa and B'Etor, the Duras sisters who provided much angst for Worf and the crew of the Enterprise in its fourth season cliffhanger, "Redemption". "Do you need to know who Lursa and B'Etor are to enjoy this lusty, busty, angry Klingon duo?" asks Braga rhetorically. "No. You will know them for who they are. Was it awkward to explain why Geordi wears a visor? Yes. But I think we did it well and that we handled each piece of exposition pretty adeptly. The film had to fit the big screen, which is more of a mood than anything else. We got to take some risks that you can't take on a week to week show and we got to do some character stuff that's really radical."

Adds Braga, "For some reason, writing this series was easier then writing a movie. I don't know why. I realized that writing a movie was a little more meticulous because it was a different medium. It was the big screen."

The film, which chronicles the Enterprise crew's attempt to stop an alien scientist from destroying the populace of an entire star system in order to complete a sinister experiment, underwent several dramatic rewrites as it evolved, needing to satisfy not only Braga and his co-writer Ron Moore, but the studio, the *Next Generation* cast (who wielded more clout than on the TV series thanks to their newly negotiated contracts), William Shatner and Rick Berman, who receives story credit for the film. "I'd be the first to tell you that the first draft needed work," says Braga. "It was the first draft of the first movie and we needed input very badly on some particular elements. There were some painful notes and the script was long and we had to cut out a large part of the storyline, but, guess what, that helped the movie a lot. There was a whole 30 page section we took out and suddenly the movie worked for the first time. Was it work by committee? No. It was notes from people who were very passionate about making it the best movie it could be — and I

• • • •

feel that it is the best movie."

Agreeing with Braga is the film's Oscar-nominated cinematographer, John Alonzo, a *Trek* novice, but a veteran DP who has helped give *Generations* its incredibly cinematic look. "It is a total departure from the kind of things that I've shot before," says Alonzo. "I thought I could bring something to it and I found [director] David Carson to have a vision for this film that I had not expected. It was not a TV box vision, it was something with grand scope and he fought very hard so we could shoot the film in cinemascope. There's also a message and a very superior performance level to the previous pictures. I think the main challenge was to keep the integrity of Gene Roddenberry's universe and not tie it into the TV series. We tried very hard to tell ourselves that this is an entirely original project which needed to be action packed and still have something to say about the condition of mankind. This is the first movie as far as I am concerned."

Not everyone agrees, however. Many of the actors reportedly expressed dissatisfaction with their roles in the feature. Michael Dorn, who had publically voiced his displeasure with the movie, was reportedly chastened by Paramount executives. During

a conclave with reporters, he said of the new film, "Worf finally gets a promotion. Besides that, there isn't much for me to do."

Dorn added about one of the film's early scenes set aboard a sailing ship based on *Mutiny on The Bounty*, championed by Berman when studio cost-cutters were looked to trim the budget. "That whole thing was something I really didn't understand. Nobody ever said anything, it just popped up. There was talk of going to Hawaii, which I thought was a great idea. The location we got is five miles off of Santa Monica."

Jonathan Frakes admits to some initial trepidation upon beginning the project, but says he's delighted with the final result. "My experience was that the script got better with each draft," he says. "I saw the dailies for the first three weeks of work that we did and I think the movie is better than any of us dared hoped it was going to be. I'm very excited about the film."

Although Patrick Stewart has publically stated he was delighted with the inclusion of members of the original cast in the film, sources report many of the *Next Gen* cast was irked over the use of classic cast members in the feature. Creatively, however, the writers felt it was

an important element to add to the feature.

"It was a creative decision that Rick, Ron, and myself made to put them in and it's just fantastic," says Braga. "It's cool to have them in the film. It's a *Next Gen* movie all the way, but the original cast plays an important part in the picture."

Adds Ron Moore, who is an avowed fan of the original series, "We knew that as soon as everyone sees that Patrick Stewart and William Shatner are in the picture, they're going to wait for the scene where these two guys say 'hi' to each other. And what are they going to say? What are they going to do? A lot of the movie succeeds and fails on how well we pull that off, so it was always a bit of an intimidating scene and it took some work. It was a real tough thing to crack."

"One thing cannot be denied," says Braga. "When Shatner plays Kirk, he *is* Kirk. It is magic. When Kirk and Picard meet, they are in an extraordinarily, strange environment that is pulling at their attentions so it's not just like two guys walking in the room saying 'pleased to meet you.' They're in an incredible *Star Trek* storyline."

With such strong protagonists at the center of the film, it was equally important

Captains Kirk (William Shatner) and Picard (Patrick Stewart) meet their maker, Great Bird of the Galaxy Gene Roddenberry (photo copyright ©1995 Albert Ortega).

to devise a worthy antagonist. "It's the kind of villain you've never seen in all of the *Next Generation* series," says Braga of Dr. Soran, played by Malcom McDowell, the malevolent El Aurian scientist determined to return to the mysterious energy ribbon in space, the Nexus. "I can't remember a more intricately drawn villain. He has to be a strong nemesis for Picard and I think that's something different you can do in movies that you can't do on TV."

The production of *Star Trek: Generations* was laced with fun for those involved; a fun that continued without pause from the television series. Rick Berman admits that it's hard to become nostalgic about the end of *The Next Generation*. "Right now, it seems like I'll be working with these people forever," he says. "It's hard to say goodbye because before the movie was out, we started working on the next movie. It is hard to say goodbye the way most shows do when they get cancelled. This is far from over."

• • • •
Directing The Generations

It should come as no small surprise to *Star Trek* fans that when *Trek* universe overlord Rick Berman set about finding a director for the new *Trek* feature, *Generations*, he seized upon the idea of hiring David Carson to take the helm of the first *Next Generation* feature.

Carson, who along with Rick Kolbe is considered among the best of the crop of *Next*

• • • •

Generation directors, has helmed some of the show's finest installments, including "The Enemy," "The Next Phase," "Yesterday's Enterprise," "Redemption" and the *Deep Space Nine* pilot, "Emissary."

For Carson, a Brit whose background is in the theater but has since gone on to direct shows like *LA Law* and *Northern Exposure*, the chance to tackle a big budget feature film was an exciting opportunity.

"I didn't approach it as one of a series," says Carson of filming the movie many have referred to simply as *Star Trek VII*. "I approached it as the first feature for the *Next Generation* and also my first feature. I didn't think of it as having a set style as there is in television, where the producers don't want you to be changing their visual style. I didn't look on this as a continuation of a series nor did I have any allegiance to what had been done before. We tried very hard not to call it *Star Trek VII*, but *Star Trek: Generations*. We saw it as a completley new departure for *Star Trek*, hopefully kicking off a new series of films."

Among those helping Carson realize his vision for the film were director of photography John Alonzo and production designer Herman Zimmerman, a veteran of two

previous *Trek* films. "We set out to tell the story as interestingly and as powerfully cinemagraphially as we possibly could by being incredibly ingenious with the sets and using the camera hand held often to give it a more fluid feel," says Carson. "It's quite tightly and dramatically shot. It's not quite as relaxed as some of the other *Star Trek* movies were. We were constantly aware that we were making a film and that it was a completely different thing we were doing from making television."

And while *Deep Space Nine*'s premiere, "Emissary" which cost over $10 million is referred to as feature quality television, Carson notes, he immediately was able to draw distinctions between the telefilm and shooting a real feature film. "Rick [Berman] had made a departure in having me do the pilot of *Deep Space Nine*. He had gone out on a limb for me there because I hadn't done any two-hour movies in this country. We worked extremely well together and when I discovered that the movie was coming along, my agent obviously put my name into the hat with all with all these other people's names. What I found out is that doing television and film are two separate organisms. The only analogy that there is, as far as I'm concerned, is that the

stretch and concentration and leap you make from doing episodic television to doing a $10 million two-hour pilot is very large. And similarly from doing movies of the week and pilots to a major $30 million film is also enormous. They are completely different in their feeling. People who work in features very often look down on the people who work in TV and, oddly enough, people have been saying to me, well, I don't suppose you'll be doing any TV now. And I say to them well, I love to be behind the camera. I love to work with actors and I love to tell stories, so I'll work anywhere that there's a film camera and somebody wants me to tell a story."

Carson adds that directing a *Star Trek* film has its own inherent challenges which make it different from shooting other types of films. "It's like doing an epic," he enthuses. "It has a scale which is epic in size. Although one strives for naturalism, it has a feeling of opera about it. It's not a naturalistic movie that takes place in prison cells or courtrooms. It takes place out in the galaxy and people behave in different ways for different reasons. So my main approach to the film and the story of the film was to realize that it is an epic. But even though it's nature is epic, I wanted to try and make sure

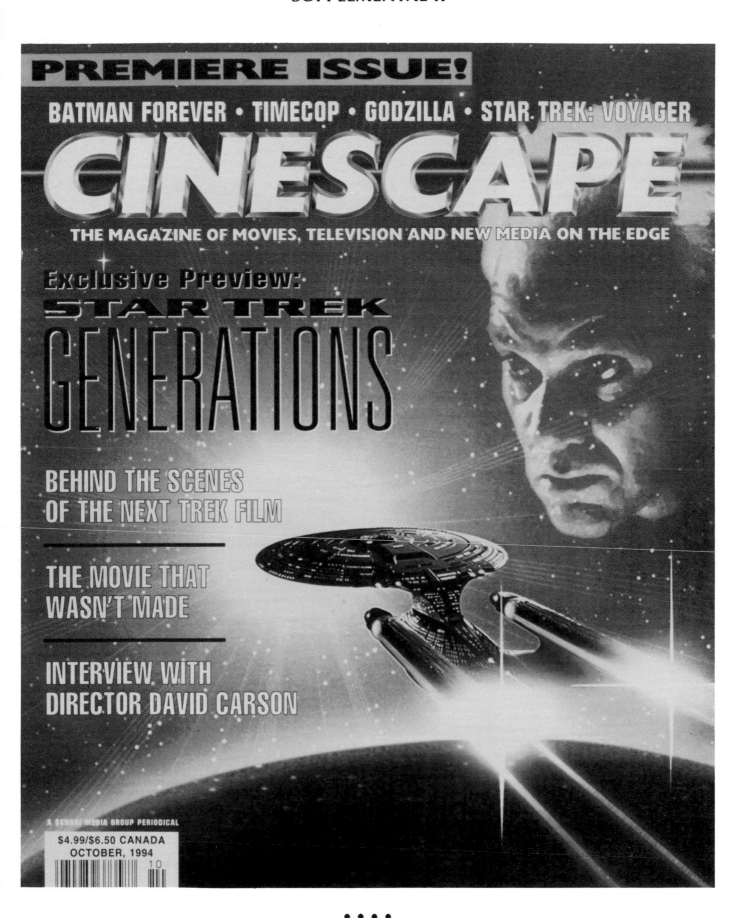

PREMIERE ISSUE!

BATMAN FOREVER • TIMECOP • GODZILLA • STAR TREK: VOYAGER

CINESCAPE

THE MAGAZINE OF MOVIES, TELEVISION AND NEW MEDIA ON THE EDGE

Exclusive Preview:
STAR TREK
GENERATIONS

**BEHIND THE SCENES
OF THE NEXT TREK FILM**

**THE MOVIE THAT
WASN'T MADE**

**INTERVIEW WITH
DIRECTOR DAVID CARSON**

A SENSAI MEDIA GROUP PERIODICAL

$4.99/$6.50 CANADA
OCTOBER, 1994

that all the aspects of it were believable. You can take things up to a line, it seems to me, and you can make them pretty preposterous and people will believe in them. But if you go beyond preposterous, it will snap people's belief barrier, if you like. And they will then start to laugh *at* the film rather than *with* the film."

It was because of Carson's concern about preserving the reality of the film that the director insisted an extensive portion of the film be deleted — a portion which involved Data seducing the Klingon sisters Lursa and B'Etor, who survive an exploding Bird of Prey and confront Riker on the planet's surface after the Enterprise crashlands. "My main objection to the conceit of Data seducing the Klingon women was that we went into an area that was preposterous and which reduced the film to farce that it would be difficult for it to recover from," says Carson. "In the end, you're dealing with a serious, heavy duty villain. And you're dealing with a couple of extremely dangerous Klingon adversaries who have to be dangerous in order to give our heroes credibility in fighting them. If, in fact, they're pussycats and really can be defeated very, very simply, what's the point? Why didn't they do that in the first

place? And although it's a funny conceit that Data has all the appendages that go with normal human beings, why would he?"

Carson adds that leaving the Klingon sisters alive also strained credibility, "If you blow a ship to pieces, it took a great stretch of the imagination for someone to discover later on, highly conveniently, that they all happened to have escaped. It strains the level of believablility. I expressed my feelings to Ron Moore and Brannon Braga and they all seemed to agree with it."

One advantage Carson had in crafting his first *Star Trek* feature was that all the casting for the film was pretty much set in stone prior to shooting. After all, the crew of the Enterprise had been galloping around the cosmos for seven years and they would all return for duty in the new film. The only source of casting anxiety was in finding the right person to play the film's black hat baddie, Dr. Soran, the mad scientist who was intent on returning to the Nexus at whatever the cost.

"It was great to have the whole thing cast," says Carson. "Then it's just up to Paramount to do the negotiation. Soran, however, was a very difficult part to cast. I think that all *Star Treks*, if they're successful, are difficult to cast because you've

got Captain Kirk, you've got Captain Picard, you've got all these other poeple like Riker, Data and Worf and then on the other side of the scale, you have this poor, lonely, innocent...well, maybe not innocent, that has to balance the film. He has to have weight and presence and charisma and he has to be able to handle words well because, of course, *Star Trek*'s language is very important to it. It's written very carefully with a lot of precision and the actors like Patrick and Jonathan and Brent are able to speak it well. You can't have someone mumble their way through their part like some well known actors are known to do. We went through discussions about many, many people and met many people from Europe and from here and we eventually settled happily on Malcolm. And then when he started to work and we started to work together, this very original and new performance came out of him. Because we're used to seeing Malcolm McDowell as this sort of off-the-wall villainous type and this is a performance he hasn't given before. It's a very interesting and very good performance."

Another challenge Carson faced was filming the epic film on a sparse fifty day shooting schedule. Says Carson, "It was just a question of having to use all of our experience to make it a good film which we could shoot pretty fast. The unfortunate thing was the fast shooting, but the good thing with the film is that it's very, very ambitious and so we had to do extremely difficult things within that fifty days. I was very fortunate to have John Alonzo as the cinematographer because, as well as being a brilliant cameraman, he's also very, very sharp. So, he was able to achieve things in a short amount of time that very few other people can. I think the cinematography in the movie is beautiful. And he was able to accomplish it very swiftly, which was an incredible help to us. It's always difficult doing difficult things in a small amount of time. I think because of the long experience that many people who worked on the film had of not just doing features but also working in television, and particularly working telling a story with the camera, which I've been doing for many years now in one medium or another, we just rose to our game and decided we'd make it absolutely the best movie in spite of the fact we only had fifty days to do it."

As for the future, the director says he looks forward to working in the feature film medium again although he doesn't necessarily plan to tackle another big budget sci-fi film so fast. "Whatever I get offered, I would like to do a good story," Carson explains. "If it's in the *Star Trek* arena or if it's in a science fiction or if it's naturalistic, I don't mind. I enjoy telling many different types of stories. I suppose, ideally, it would be very, very nice for me to be able to do something that was completely different. This film is on a very big scale. I love stories where you lay out clues for the audience and the audience tries to tie them together while you have your characters trying to tie them together at the same time. And you try and stay ahead of the audience. That's the name of the game."

Meeting The Press

At the time of the release of Star Trek: Generations, *certain members of the cast and crew took the time to meet with the press to promote the film. What follows are edited transcripts of those conversations with Great Bird Rick Berman, director David Carson and stars Patrick Stewart, Brent Spiner, Malcolm McDowell and William Shatner.*

• • • •

RICK BERMAN
(Producer)

Q.

Were you the one who decided to use Patrick Stewart in the first place?

A.

No, but I was partially responsible.

Q.

Because I thought that was a brave choice. I mean, here he was a British, classically trained....

A.

Actually, when we were casting for Captain Picard, one of my fellow producers, a guy named Bob Justman, had seen Patrick Stewart give a lecture at UCLA and he was very impressed with him. He had also seen him on *I, Claudius* on PBS. So, he brought him in to meet Roddenberry and Roddenberry's reaction was, "A bald, middle-aged British guy? You've got to be kidding" and he said, "No." This was all before I met these guys. It was a few weeks before I met them. So, then when I came in — I knew who Patrick was but when I came in, Justman, who had known Roddenberry for years — he had worked on the original series with him — said to me, "Once Gene makes a decision, he never changes his mind and don't even think about asking him again to talk about this — to discuss this English actor." But I was living in this kind of benign ignorance of all that and I had nothing to lose. So, I started bugging Gene about it because we really weren't finding anybody who was close. Justman used to say, "You can't do that. He has made up his mind. You can't do that." But I just kept nudging him and nudging him and finally he agreed to consider Patrick and he changed his mind. So, I didn't discover him but I helped push Gene over to our side.

Q.

Rick, tell us about the last year for you. Do you sort of feel like you are coming towards the end of the tunnel as *Voyager* starts production, *Deep Space Nine* is continuing, you have been through the finale of the first show, then through this film?

A.

Every week I always say to myself, this week is going to be a bitch but next week things are really going to lighten up. I said that when we wrapped the film a couple of weeks ago and when we finally locked it, I said, "This is going to be great," but for instance this week we have to lock the pilot on *Voyager* which we are in our last week of editing on. I've got all these screenings and premieres to go to on this movie and I'm moving this week. In fact, Wednesday, I am going to go to work in the morning, go to the cast and crew screening, which is our first big screening of the film, and then go home to a different house. It has been a busy year, but to me I like to think it is always going to calm down, but it really never does. After this week and after the movie opens,

Rick Berman and Michael Piller, co-creators of Deep Space Nine *and* Voyager *(photo copyright ©1995 Albert Ortega).*

Voyager is in production and *Deep Space Nine* is in production, we will begin discussions on stories for the next movie. So, it will continue to be busy, I think.

Q.

They are already talking a second movie?

A.

Paramount is talking to me about the second movie. So we are negotiating things and we are already working on some story ideas.

Q.

Depending on gross?

A.

If nobody goes to see this movie, probably they won't want to do another one. I have a funny feeling that people are going to see this movie.

Q.

In terms of *Voyager*, was it a conscious decision to make the premise different than what had come before?

A.

The difference is very important to us. When we developed *Voyager*, we didn't want to give them a show that was identical to *The Next Generation*. It's also good for us because as storytellers, it is very hard to just keep doing the same thing. So, we made *Deep Space Nine* and *Voyager* different primarily to keep us fresh and hopefully to keep the audience interested.

Q.

What do you think is the ongoing appeal of *Star Trek*?

A.

I think there is a few reasons for that — I'm only answering this kind of quickly because on the television version of this [junket] yesterday, I was asked this question about 45 times so I got my answer down.

Q.

Only 45 ....

A.

No, no. There were 66 actual-ly. *Star Trek*, I think, foremost is a show that portrays a better future. It gives a sense of hope for the future, which was Roddenberry's whole version of the 23rd and later the 24th century and I think that is something that makes people feel good. I also think that *Star Trek* is a television show about a family, about a group of people who were good to one another and who are positive, loving people who were off on an adventure, exploring strange new worlds. I also think that *Star Trek* has become a part of the American culture. You would be hard pressed to find someone who has never heard beaming someone somewhere or warp speed or photon torpedoes or Klingons or any of these things that are a part of *Star Trek*. I think there is a certain famil-iarity and comfort in that.

Q.

How difficult has it been creat-ing *Voyager* while also chang-ing the premise in the sense that we're coming home instead of going out there? Did that create a different set of challenges?

A.

Yeah, again, we wanted

THE OFFICIAL MAGAZINE OF THE SCI-FI CHANNEL

RETAILER: DISPLAY UNTIL FEBRUARY 28

SCI-FI
ENTERTAINMENT

SCI-FI CHANNEL

WPS 36021 Science Fiction Age

Star Trek:
VOYAGER

WILLIAM SHATNER & TEKWAR

CLIVE BARKER:
Hellraiser IV,
Candyman 2 &
Lord of Illusions

FOREVER KNIGHT RETURNS

TWILIGHT ZONE QUIZ

Sci-Fi Channel
Schedule Inside!

$3.50
CAN: $4.50; UK: £2.25
FEBRUARY 1995

Deep Space Nine*'s Avery Brooks and Nana Visitor with Majel Barrett Roddenberry at the premiere of* Star Trek: Generations *(photo copyright ©1995 Albert Ortega).*

Voyager to be different. So we made it different primarily in three ways. First of all, Gene Roddenberry didn't want conflict amongst his characters. He thought that was a problem which is great, but it doesn't help writing drama because conflict is what drives that. So, we are always trying — without breaking Gene's rules — to find ways to put conflict into it. In *Deep Space Nine* we did it by putting people in uncomfortable environments with others who were not Starfleet people who were constantly giving them aggravation. In *Voyager* there is a group called the Maquis, which are a group of human freedom fighters or terrorists — depending on how you look at them — and we have those but they are well-meaning people in a way. We start our first premiere two-hour episode off with the starship Voyager chasing a bunch of these Maquis. Eventually they both end up on the far side of the galaxy and they end up having to join together because one of the ships is destroyed and these Maquis become Starfeet officers, but there will always be some conflict between them. That gave us something new and unique. Secondly, we have our people 70 years away from home, not necessarily spending their lives getting home, but looking for ways home but while doing it, exploring space. The most unique thing about that is it enables us to no longer be in contact with Starfeet. It's not like we can call home for instructions all the time. We are on our own, which is another thing. The final thing was that we put a woman at the helm, which was something that we thought it was time to do and gives the show a slightly different edge.

Q.

The quote "Time is the fire in which we burn" worked out very well in the movie, I thought.

A.

When we were developing a story about people obsessed with time and people obsessed with their own mortality, we pulled out a lot of quotes and a lot of things that seemed to be relevant to the story. This Delmore Schwartz quote kind of hit it right on the head. One of the actors, I'm not sure which, kept insisting that that quote was from Shakespeare. I remember going back and saying, "It's Delmore Schwartz" and everybody thought I was kidding.

Q.

This film to me appears to be particularly lush and lavish in its production, the lighting and cinematography and special effects, it seems to me to be about the best of the entire movie series in terms of production, and I wanted to know if you could talk about that. The choice of ILM and conceptualizing the special effects.

A.

Well, one of the benefits we have had by doing this television series for so many years is having put together a team of remarkable people. Our visual effects teams, who have been working with us for nearly eight years, now are among the best there are. We don't have a facility like ILM does in Northern California, but we have terrific people who are always on the cutting edge of having to go about doing this stuff. That is always because on television you never have the budget to do it properly, so you always have to find new ways of doing it so you can get it done. So, we were in the position to be able to use those people. We have used ILM before. ILM is one of a number of places that bid on this job

that ended up getting it, and we worked very closely with them for the last year and a half on all of the opticals. There are over 200 opticals in this movie, which is a lot. The optical budget on this film — although I'm not supposed to tell you what it is — is higher than any of the other *Star Trek* movies. Part of it is like the old Avis thing, you know, we try harder. Being involved in television, we spend our lives fighting time and fighting budgets to do things in a small way which, of course, we do, always dreaming and wishing that we could do things properly. This was our opportunity to do things properly. John Alonzo was our cinematographer, who was terrific; and David Carsen had a vision that we worked on very carefully to be sure we all agreed on what the movie was going to look like.

Q.

Is Whoopi Goldberg going to be involved in future projects?

A.

You mean beyond this movie?

Q.

Yes.

A.

Well, she is terrific in this film and I'm sure that she will be....

Q.

Did she ask not to be credited?

A.

Yes, she did, which I think is somewhat common when big stars have smaller roles in films.

Q.

There seems to have been so many stories in the press and they were attacking you, attacking the movie, attacking *Voyager* on a weekly basis. It feels like one of those situations where *Star Trek* has reached this level now, let's try to knock it down. Did you feel that way at all?

A.

Yeah, a little bit. There were always rumors. We lived with rumors for years with the television show because *Star Trek* is so popular and it means so much to so many people. They are so passionate about it, you get gossip and you get rumors,

but it wasn't until we made a movie that things were getting printed in national magazines. There were stories printed about the test screenings that we had that were totally false, just made up by somebody! There were stories about this Genevieve Bujold thing which were just 100% false. Not even somebody misinterpreting something. I was just envisioning 16 year old disgruntled kids who for some reason didn't get an autograph or something like that, sitting down on the Internet at 3:00 in the morning, typing out some kind of a story and the next day it is in a national newspaper. It's kind of scary, but we have had a love/hate relationship with *Entertainment Weekly*. They do incredible things — very, very favorable things and then they will write an article and very often they will take these things and they will base them on totally incorrect hearsay. The greatest thing is we traced this. You have a 15 year old who writes something on the Internet and the next day it is in a tabloid, but then *Entertainment Weekly* will have read it in the tabloid and then all of a sudden a major newspaper will say that we read it in *Entertainment Weekly*. All of a sudden you have read something in five different sources that was all totally uncorroborated non-

sense that was just some disgruntled person making something up. That was frustrating for us, but there has been a lot more good publicity that we have had than bad.

Q.

How did you originally get involved in *Star Trek* and did you know what you were getting into at the time?

A.

No, I certainly didn't know what I was getting into at the time. I was a producer of films and television and a writer here in New York. I moved to California in 1984 and I ended up working as a Development Executive for Paramount Pictures. I was made a Vice President in less than two years of being in LA and one day somebody decided that they were going to do a new *Star Trek* television series. I was the lowest man on the totem pole, I was the lowest vice president and I think they figured that Roddenberry was known as being such a pain in the ass they would give this one to me. "Go over there to Building B, you can have him." So, I went and developed a wonderful rapport with Gene. I had done a lot of travelling because I had worked with the United Nations on making films for them, and I sat down and had lunch with Gene one day and we had a lot in common. For two people who had nothing in common, we had a lot in common. The next day I got a phone call from his lawyer — who was also like his personal manager — who asked to have lunch with me. So, it was like two lunches in a row. This is going to be fun and he said we would like you to leave your job as Paramount Vice President. We would like you to come work for us on the show. So, this all happened in two days. It was risky for me because this was a syndicated television show, which one hour dramatic shows were unheard of as being successful; which was science fiction which at that point was something that nobody was really embracing, and it was a sequel. It was three strikes against me to start. So, I thought about it for about three minutes and said, yes, because I didn't enjoy being a studio executive. I wanted to go back to producing and I started working with Gene and after about the first year, he got the show steered in the right direction and trusted me and had confidence that I was not going to try to fix *Star Trek*. He was constantly running into people who wanted to fix *Star Trek*.

He was confident that I was going to try and keep his vision relatively clear. So, he stepped back kind of quickly because he was not feeling too well at that point. It is very difficult producing episodic television. It is very long hours. He sort of gave it to me.

Q.

Is it true that Roddenberry's ashes were brought into space aboard one of the space shuttles?

A.

I think, in fact, they weren't scattered, they were brought up and it was a tiny little pinch of them and it was something that was done on the slide because I don't think you are supposed to do that. But one of the astronauts who knew Gene, I believe, took a tiny little bit up on one of the shuttle trips and gave it back to Majel [Barrett Roddenberry], or at least that is what I was told.

Q.

Majel has been involved in all the versions of *Star Trek*. Did you use her in the film?

A.

Yeah. We didn't want to do it without her, so there is a sequence when — right before the saucer separates, when everybody is evacuating the ship, you hear the computer and that is Majel.

Q.

A lot of the cast members seemed to not have much to do. Obviously you have to get the Captain stories in and you can only get so many people involved, but Spot the cat has more screen time than many of the cast does You had to make those decisions, but these are people that you worked with for seven years. In the day to day series, you can say, "Okay, you're not in this episode, but you'll be in the next one." Is that the same thing here — "You won't be in this movie, but you'll be in the next one." How do deal with the egos and certain feelings and people coming to you begging for more? Begging to get on *Deep Space Nine* or *Voyager*?

A.

Spot, the cat gave me a lot of trouble. We have the unique situation in that this was a movie that had fifteen roles in it that had already been cast before we wrote the movie. You are not dealing with actors who read for a role and get it and they are happy. You have actors who have the role already, who feel they know more about the character than you do, and who undoubtedly will feel underpaid and under-used and so that is something you've got to deal with very sensitively. We have seven characters from *The Next Generation*, Whoopi is eight, three characters from the original series. That is eleven and a couple of others. You've got like 15 characters. So the question becomes — you can't have 15 stars in the movie and as this story evolved, we ended up with Kirk and Picard and Data having the three major arcs in this film and Soran, the guest star, our villain. So, what you try to do is you try to create minor storylines or scenes that the other actors will have that will showcase them to some degree. It is frustrating. It is frustrating for the actors and sometimes those things will be minimized in the cutting room, not because that is the way it was planned, but because when you are pasting the movie in the cutting room and you've got to lose things and shorten things, you end up bringing things down. LeVar

Walter Koenig (above) reprised his role of Chekov and James Doohan (right) brings Scotty to life one more time in Generations *(photos copyright ©1995 Albert Ortega).*

had a wonderful scene that was dramatically short, not because of LeVar but because of the pasting of the movie. I think if you look at the original *Star Trek* movies, you will see numerous films where a number of the actors had small parts. It is part of the game. When you have an ensemble in any one given movie, it is going to just feature certain people and there were hurt feelings, but I worked diligently with every one of our actors on their parts, because these people know these characters very well. They played them for over seven years and we worked with them and everybody had notes. Especially with Patrick, Brent and Bill, we made a lot of changes and we made a lot of accommodations and they helped. They made it better.

• • • •

Q.

I think some of us are wondering why some of the original series cast members appeared and some of the others didn't.

A.

That's very simple. When we developed this story, originally we just wanted to introduce the original cast in a prologue in the beginning of the movie, kind of a farewell for these guys and then when we started developing the story, we realized there was a way to bring Kirk back into it and that he could have an arc that would remain at the end, and that was the script that we wrote. So, when we brought it to Leonard and when we brought it to DeForest Kelley, they both looked at it and they had what amounted to elaborate cameos. I don't think they even had ten lines in the picture and for them they felt that they had said the proper good-bye in *Star Trek VI*, a film that was designed to be the last *Star Trek* movie. If you recall, if you saw that movie, it ended with each one of their signatures, the actor's name appearing on the screen saying good-bye. For DeForest Kelley and for Leonard I think the feeling was that they had left the *Star Trek* series of films in the proper fashion and they didn't want to come back to do it in a short piece. With Shatner it was different because he had a role that he really thought would be a challenge to him and would be a lot of fun.

Q.

Are there plans to bring either the original cast or *The Next Generation* cast on to *Deep Space Nine?*

A.

We are always playing around with those things and we have done that over the years. DeForest Kelley, Scotty and Spock have been on *The Next Generation*, so we have managed to do that. Whether it continues, we'll have to wait and see.

Q.

In regards to the reshooting of the ending, Malcolm McDowell said that as they shot it originally, they knew it was anticlimactic in a sense. That shooting Kirk in the back wasn't exciting enough for all that had come before in the movie. Was that part of the reason for the reshoot — that it just wasn't an exciting ending for an exciting movie?

A.

I don't think that we knew it was anticlimactic. We knew that we had less time to do it. This was at the very end of the shoot and we were running out of time — that's what the movie is about, right? And we didn't have the time to do it properly. When we came back and screened the film for a test audience, we had a wonderful reception to the movie, but the test audience — and more importantly — all of us saw six and a half minutes of the film — the stuff that you guys saw that is on the bridge — that we felt was not as exciting as it could be and we were blessed in that Paramount said to us, "If you want to go back and redo it, go back and redo it." So, there was a part of us that kept saying we have to go back to that dreadful mountain in Nevada, but we did. We went back and reshot that six and a half minutes and we made it better. You know, again you were talking about the press and gossip and things — I read incredible things. I read that we had terrible reports [from the screening], which was completely incorrect. It was one of the highest testing first-tested movies that Paramount had ever done. I read we were doing it to alter Kirk's fate — to make Kirk's fate more ambiguous. Totally incorrect things that somebody just makes up and all of a sudden the next day you read about it on the front page of the entertainment section. We went back because there was this six and a half minute segment that we wanted to punch up and make a little bit more exciting.

Q.

Didn't Paramount do the same thing with *Fatal Attraction*? It was a great movie with a weak ending in which they said let's reshoot and it turned it into a $300 million movie?

A.

Well, in the test screening we sensed that this six and half minutes I am talking about didn't get the same amount of enthusiasm, but to me this is an example in favor of the testing procedure. We tested the movie. It got a wonderful response. There was one area that seemed a little disappointing — not disappointing — a *little* disappointing, and we went back and fixed it, which kinds of shows the persistence ....

Q.

There wasn't that luxury in *Star Trek V*. Paramount didn't like the movie so it just kind of threw it out there to fend for itself.

A.

So, it ended up working out for the best. *Clear and Present Danger* is a very big movie — it is one of the top grossing movies of the year. They went back to Mexico to reshoot a bunch of scenes. You don't read about it in the paper because it is a normal process.

Q.

In *Star Trek II* Spock was dead but he wasn't dead. Is Kirk really dead?

Somehow it seems appropriate for Wiliam Shatner to be posing with a car of the future (photo copyright ©1995 Albert Ortega).

are shooting our fourth episode right now. We are in discussions about the next movie and that's plenty for me. In the television business, people work under this horrible spectra of never knowing if you are going to get cancelled tomorrow. If you have a full year commitment, it is considered a relaxed state. We have television shows that we know are going to run for many years. I've got a movie opening this week that I'm pretty secure is going to do very well, and we are going to start developing another one. So, as far as the future is concerned, I would love to take a few days off. I've been working a lot of weekends.

A.

Is Kirk really dead?

Q.

I mean, he is dead, but....

A.

He is not here today.

Q.

Will you swear that there is no possible way he will ever come back?

A.

No, I will not.

Q.

What are you striving for?

A.

That's like saying, beyond your work and your leisure time, what is your future? Right now we are continuing with *Deep Space Nine* and *Voyager*. *Voyager*, I think, is going to be really terrific. We put together a remarkable cast and it's going really, really well. We

• • • •

....
DAVID CARSON
(Director)

Q.

Why did you cut the scene with Malcolm McDowell torturing LeVar Burton?

A.

The thing about this scene was that basically in the scheme of things when we put the movie together, it was too long. It said what it needed to say three times in slightly different ways and it said it in the center of the film, where you needed to be moving more swiftly than we were able to. So, what we decided to do in the end is not go into a great torture scene with Geordi screaming and yelling and things all happening and people pressing things and touching his heart and stuff like that, but to give the impression that this extremely evil man is now going to torture him and make him feel extraordinary unhappy and uncomfortable, which is what we ended up with. The scene repeated its theme as interrogation scenes often do. "Now, I want you to tell me what Captain Picard knows about Thilithium." "I'm not going to tell you."

"Well, I want you to tell me." "I'm not going to tell." "Well, I'm going to torture you." "I'm still not going to tell you." "Well, I still want you to tell me."

Q.

Can't you tell that from the script initially?

A.

No, sometimes you can't tell these things from the script. That scene itself contains some of the basis of Malcolm's character and one of the tragedies about cutting the end of the scene was that we lost some of the detail of his character. This is how movies get made. You cannot possibly tell sometimes unless you are an incredible genius, and even then they tend to reshoot just as much as anybody else does — you can't tell how the structure of your movie physically is going to work out differently from on the page.

Q.

What was it like working with William Shatner?

A.

You mean playing Captain Kirk?

Q.

No — yeah, either way.

A.

Well, let me talk about him playing Captain Kirk. As a man, from what little I know of him, he is a multi-faceted, multi-talented individual. He has his hands in so many different piles, not all entertainment. I mean he has achievements in dealing with horses and things like that which seem to be quite remarkable for somebody who doesn't know very much about horses. So, he seems to be a multi-talented individual. However, when he walks onto the bridge of the Enterprise with his costume on and his makeup on, he is Captain Kirk. He brings with him the remarkable legacy. He is Captain Kirk and he doesn't walk onto the set and fool about — I don't mean fool about like other actors do but have a good time as Bill Shatner. He walks onto the set and he is Captain Kirk and the eyes and the cameras follow him and the people have

William Shatner and Patrick Stewart first met each other at Creation's "Two Captains" convention (photo copyright ©1995 Karen Witkowski).

grown up with the legend of *Star Trek* react when he walks on. I mean, they really do because here they are on the Enterprise-B. They have never been on it before and he is Captain Kirk. Here is the power and strength of this incredible legend. He is an icon of American mythology. He is a hero but he happens to be walking about amongst us when he puts that uniform on. As an actor, he is the most wonderfully talented and imaginative actor — full of ideas, always wanting to contribute and join in and discuss and elaborate and fully round out what he is doing. Very willing to experiment and try different things even though his character — which he has created, of course — has not done such things before. Very interested in expanding his view of Captain Kirk. As you can see, I like him a lot and got on with him very well. It was really a pleasure working with him.

Q.

Tell me about the difference in directing between Stewart and Shatner, just in the fact that you were familiar with one and not the other, and also whether or not it changed your directing of Patrick working with him on film as opposed to the series.

A.

One of the director's jobs is to create the atmosphere on the set for the actors to do their best work. In most stories, the performance is paramount. Everybody talks about the special effects and stuff like that in *Star Trek*. *Star Trek* is a relationship-oriented piece of entertainment. Those are the most important things. So, therefore, we can have many special effects — and we have 220 of them in the movie — but without these performances and without the seriousness in which the performances relate to the themes, we are sunk. Now, my inclination is always to treat each actor totally differently. I attempt to talk to them in their language. Find out what their language is. Certainly I don't talk to Bill Shatner in an American accent, but I try to tune in to what he is doing so I can swiftly communicate with him. So, the difference between working with Patrick and Bill, is that I have a shorthand with Patrick. We worked together. We understand each other. I can communicate with him in ways that are invariably much shorter, crisper and we understand each other and lock on and he talks back to me. We have a shorthand and that grows with

your acquaintance with an actor. With Bill we immediately locked on well together. We understood each other, but things just take that little bit longer. These are tiny, tiny things with dealing with an actor. Some actors love conflict. Some creators like to create the conflict. Actors are no different from anybody like that. These two actors were basically professionals who seemed to long to work with each other. When they came onto the set, they were just a delight. They were full of ideas. They were ready to work. They exchanged ideas between themselves and me and we had a great time. We had none of the anticipated furor or egos and stuff like that.

Q.

Obviously the two characters have opposite personalities....

A.

Well, in a way Picard and Kirk — although they are totally separate — are like two sides of the same coin. They complement and although they overlap in their various skills and areas, the twinkle with which Bill Shatner does everything— that Kirk does everything — and the seriousness in

Alan Ruck, perhaps best known as Cameron in Ferris Bueller's Day Off *and an annoying tourist in* Speed, *portrayed the inept Enterprise-B captain John Harriman (photo copyright ©1995 Albert Ortega).*

which Picard does everything are sort of like opposites that attract. I mean Kirk with gay abundance leaps into the prey with a twinkle in his eyes and quip on his lips which, if you like, is an old-fashioned heroic way of doing things. Picard enters things seriously and perhaps with the same sort of excitement and twinkle in his eye, but there is no usual quip on the lips. He is dealing with things very, very strongly. What we did in the movie when we dealt with the Enterprise-B and the Enterprise - D, was we tried to treat the Enterprise-B and the people in it as if we were dealing with a period; we were consciously doing a film that was 100 years older than the other one and we tried to light it differently and use our cameras slightly differently and it seems to have worked because people have commented to me that it was slightly more old-fashioned than the Enterprise-D. We tried to make a difference between them, but, in fact, when you put Kirk and Picard together in the same setting at the same time, the main difference is one of fashion. The kind of trousers that Kirk wears as opposed to what Picard wears, but I don't see a difference in here is a 60's style and a 90's style. Here is a hero from that particular era and here is a hero from this particular era.

Q.

Was it difficult to direct the scene where Kirk dies?

A.

It wasn't difficult, no. The difficult thing about it or the challenging thing about it is not that he dies but how he dies. And the expectations of everybody who has been with him in his various mythical exploits over the last 30 years, have about the death of a hero. The hero dies and he has to die correctly. That was the most challenging thing to work out. I think, for example, a part of the mythology has been when Kirk dies, he dies alone. In this movie he died alone, but because this is about handing of the torch, obviously when he dies, he passes the torch in many ways. His mortality, which is what the film is about, comes into the new generation, the next generation. So, he had to die with Picard and one of the differences we made between the ending that we created to start with and then the change that we made, was that I tried to create this barrier around Kirk so that Picard could not get at him and he couldn't touch him. He was under all this incredible amount of metal

which was tangled and he was inside. So, I started in a way where you see Picard coming down and you see this thing in a distance and then you see him for a long time looking through the metal and see what the damage is and he doesn't see Kirk. We reveal Kirk right at the end when Picard comes to look at him and you see the distance between them and the two men are incredibly well separated. So, we tried to be truthful to those things and yet looked at our own needs. I think with the performance that Bill gave and that we worked on for that week, it was a very delicate and moving performance.

Q.

But, in fact, you did reshoot it based on audience response?

A.

We reshot it because we wanted to — having seen it much in the same vein that I was talking about earlier. I mean, what an amazing thing to be able to do. Do it better and bigger and, yeah, this is a wonderful film is what they said but the interesting thing about the two endings — and I don't believe it is any secret because I understand that you can get the first script from somewhere and look at it on the Internet — was that the same basic ideas that we used in the first version are in the second version. In other words, that Captain Kirk gives his life for 230 million people. He saves the situation like that. He dies trying to save the universe and he dies with Captain Picard. He uses his strength and his ability to leap into battle with a smile on his lips and all that sort of thing to physically attack and deal with Soran, who we have seen already in the film, Picard can't deal with. He is head-butted down a levine. So, when he comes back, he needs Kirk's physical skills and his ability to deal with things physically while Picard goes and deals with the launcher. But throughout the film we had moving scenes of highs and lows, and the simplicity of this ending was governed by this 50 day schedule that we had to deal with. I mean we had to bring it in in 50 days in order to keep the budget down so we could do this huge effort. The only way we could get away with doing this effort and not spend $100 million was to do it quickly and do it in 50 days. So, we had to make some simplicity work on our side, but to make a long story short, when we got to the

end and discovered that we had these huge calamities in our ending which was satisfactory and was good and true and was simple, it wasn't satisfying enough. It didn't go that whole way to satisfy. So, we went as the film makers to Sherry Lansing and said we are very anxious about the ending. We would like to do more. We know from *Casablanca* endings have been reshot, so it is nothing new and I thought that perhaps with a bit of luck they would let me have the actors and bits of metal and we could get on a building on top of Paramount somewhere and do it and I would get a day to shoot it if I was lucky. I thought I could change it enough to make it more powerful and stronger, but when Sherry saw the film, she looked at it and said, "This is a wonderful film. Let's go for the ending. Let's go and expand it and get the guys together more." So, what we did though was instead of having Kirk nose to nose constantly to Soran, which is how the first one was, we put him in a different sort of physical danger which was the bridge and the danger was created by Soran but he then had to leap to the bridge. So, we just changed it and expanded it. But we didn't throw one ending away and rewrite it. As I said before, what an incredibly

fortunate thing to have happened to us.

Q.

Why didn't Whoopi Goldberg take credit on this film?

A.

Rick would probably know more about this than I do, but I believe it was her request that she should be not used as the mega star in this. She says in her one woman shows it is her attachment to *Star Trek* and her belief in *Star Trek* from when she was a child that made her want to be in it and she asked for a role to be written in this film for her but she doesn't want to appear above the title as a Whoopi Goldberg movie. I remember a very famous episode called "Yesterday's Enterprise" and that came about because I was scheduled to do an episode and I didn't know which one it was. Suddenly Whoopi was free and they said, "Quick, get Whoopi over here." They didn't have a script. So, there we were with seven days to start shooting with no script, but we did have Whoopi, because whenever she becomes free and she is able to give us a day or two, she generously does that because

Finally, a little more of Guinan's background was revealed in Generations (Whoopi Golberg photo copyright ©1995 Albert Ortega).

she wants to be a part of it. She feels it is important to her life so I can understand her saying — and I think it is fair too — that she not be used as this juggernaut, which she is, to sell a movie.

Q.

Why weren't some of the other people from the original show cast?

A.

Because only two people were written to be with Captain Kirk. George Takei in a way was in the show. Sulu's daughter was in it, which I thought was a wonderful, wonderful way of continuing the generations and speaking about mortality. See, it was more important for us I think to deal with our theme, which is about mortality, the handing on of torches, the passing from generation to generation. To have a child of one of the originals on board the ship, actually I think makes a greater point than producing everybody from the last series and indeed as the publicity says, it is a story about two captains and the passing of the torch from one generation to another. But to have the entire old cast makes it become a little bit like a boy's club or all girl's club instead of

telling the story. We wanted to have a point. It wasn't just a lark and romp in space. I mean, very deliberately another one of the scenes that we cut from the movie that I think everybody now knows about is a scene which starts with Bill parachuting out of orbital sky-diving into a hay field and land-ing undignified and Scotty run-ning along behind him. "What are you doing? You are too old to be doing this sort of thing" which is very much like how some of the old movies started, you know. It started with a joke and all of that and as I said to Bill, the point about this movie is not that you are going off to do deeds of daring for two hours or so, therefore, it will be good to have a scene where you are shown as a human being and it is funny and it is sort of interesting. In this movie, the first time you see Captain Kirk, he is Captain Kirk. He is a hero. He is the folkloric figure because it is his move-ment to that inclination to his death and the passing from one generation to another, but it is important in the story. So, that is why we decided to set it up as we did. We wanted Captain Kirk and we wanted to suggest the rest of the generation by having two of his officers with him. There was some argument about who they were going to be, but that is why we came to that decision.

• • • •

Generations live! William Shatner and Patrick Stewart share a New York City stage (photo copyright ©1995 Karen Witkowski).

• • • •
PATRICK STEWART
(Captain Jean Luc Picard)

Q.

Is this the most massive press event you have been around?

A.

Oh, yes. I've never done this before. I'm a virgin and yesterday was one of the most curious days of my life. We were doing broadcast interviews and I think it was very tough — tough on the inter-

viewers too, I think.

Q.

You have done some courageous things in your career. Leaving the RSC and coming to the U.S. What was the toughest thing you ever did?

A.

Taking this job I used up every single minute of the five days that Paramount gave me to make up my mind about the TV series — not the movie. I didn't have many doubts about

the movie, but in 1987 for the first time in quite a number of years, I felt that my career was moving in a way that I could hardly control. I liked what was happening to me. I liked the work that was coming in. I had been achieving a certain amount of success in areas that were new to me and I was looking forward to the end of the 80's, spending my life mostly on the stage. In fact, I was in the middle of a very successful production of *Who's Afraid of Virginia Wolf.* I think I made the right choice, but it was very, very difficult and I went right to the wire in making the decision. The last couple of days I talked with many people and asked them what I should do and the last person I went to see was the screenwriter/director Tom Ritman. I said, "Tell me what to do. I don't know what I should do about this job." He said, "I think you should come to America. I think you should work in Hollywood for a period of time. All the other work will still be there when you are done. It won't go away and I think you should come to the United States and have a lot of fun." I wasn't to know it then, but of course, fun was the one thing that was to characterize the next seven years because I was to laugh more in the next seven years than I had in the previous 45.

Q.

So, you don't regret the decision?

A.

No. There would be nothing that I would change. Even now looking back on seven years on the series, if I had known it would have been seven years, I would not have signed up. It was just too big of a chunk out of my life. We used to sit around and play games — Brent, Jonathan, all

of us projecting how long it would run and we would settle between two to three years maximum. Oh, it shows how naive you are.

Q.

So, you actually did sign a seven year contract?

A.

No, I signed a six year contract. I was so innocent, I didn't realize that if I agreed to do the pilot, I was in effect signing a six year contract. That's the way it is for a TV series. When actors go to network, you are making a commitment and it is very much a one-sided commitment too. No, I would not have accepted the offer, but now that I can see it from this point of view now, seven years later, everything worked out just fine.

Q.

Was it harder working on the stage?

A.

The only time in my life that I have worked harder than in the seven years of *The Next*

Generation series was when I was seventeen and I worked for a building contractor who, feeling that I needed to be built up, used to insist that I mixed cement by hand. There was no other job that has taxed me physically than *The Next Generation* did. Largely because of the nature of my role, I was there for long days — 14, 15, 16, 17 or 18 hours. Although as a director I hold the record for the longest day on the set, but that was the day I was a director and not an actor.

Q.

How long?

A.

The crew call was at 7:00 a.m. and I wrapped at 2:35 in the morning.

Q.

Would you have been willing to do a couple more?

A.

No.

• • • •

Q.

Some people say that you were one of the main reasons the series was cancelled.

A.

So, I am told. I am flattered by those remarks, that people should think that I have that much power. In fact, Paramount and I had an open arrangement for an eighth season and this time the option was on both sides, which is a little unusual. As it happened, the studio pulled the show. I was never consulted and I feel their timing was perfect. I liked the idea that we would end the series when we were on top and the very final episode that we did was one of the best that we had done in the whole show. Everyone was ready. I started to fear that I as an actor might start repeating myself. Days were not as interesting and as exciting as they had been and I was looking for fresh fields and pastures new. I wish we had not had to go into the movie quite so quickly as we did. We had four days off — I had four days off between wrapping the series and stepping on board the Lady Washington in Santa Monica Bay. Luckily I did not have to do too much character research before we went.

Q.

How would you say the characters of Picard and Kirk are different from each other?

A.

Well, I don't know what it feels like to be Captain Kirk. I know what it feels like to be Captain Picard. In many respects it is the very same view to be Patrick Stewart, because the edges have become somewhat blurred now. Where one leaves off and the other one begins, I don't know. Over the years a lot of what I believe, what interests me, a lot of what gets my attention has gone into Jean Luc Picard and a certain amount of him has hopefully rubbed off on me. Perhaps, in essence, the differences would seem to be pretty clear. Picard is essentially a negotiator, a talker, a diplomat, and Kirk is very much a man of action. He would throw a punch first and ask questions afterwards.

Q.

There's that moment when Kirk says to Picard "I thought you were going to get the mis-sile," and you said, "Oh, I've changed my mind," like you want to have in on the fun. Sort of more hands-on.

A.

That's right. I changed my mind. Captain's Perogative. It is as though there is a little of Captain Kirk rubbing off in that moment. There were more jokes which are no longer in the movie. I'm sad about that, but there were some other elements of humor and ironic comments and so forth. Some little puns largely to do with play on the word bridge. I think at the time it was probably not a place to be ironic. I'm told that the cinema audiences cheer when he says, "Don't you talk to me like that. I was saving the galaxy when your grandfather was still in diapers." It's a funny line and, of course, it reverberates in a multitude of different ways, too, because it's not only Kirk speaking to Picard but it is the actor Bill Shatner speaking to Patrick Stewart. I thought that was charming.

Q.

How did that feel when the two of you were working together? Obviously there were various reports about conflicts, but the fact is on the series you were clearly in charge — the man — the central figure — the captain. Here you are in almost some ways a co-equal, maybe even, some would argue, slightly lesser than Kirk. How does that feel?

A.

It felt absolutely incredible. I'm very, very satisfied with how it has turned out in the movie. I had been the most passionate voice for this being a truly transitional movie. Three years ago when rumors of a feature film was first floating around, I said this film must include as many members of the original crew as possible. Find some way of bringing all of us together. Not only would I feel it would be missing a simply unique filming opportunity to have the two crews side by side — and I do regret it's not the entire original cast, but wouldn't it have been wonderful to have one scene and have both crews together in the same room? Well, of course, it is Star Trek and that may still happen because anything can happen on *Star Trek*. When it became a reality that there would be a role for Bill and originally, of course, Spock was written into the movie and Bones — they were

all there — I was so anxious that Bill should find the role interesting and that he should want to do it. It would have been a bitter disappointment if he had pulled out. But once we got working together and I began to tune in on to just how Bill plays this guy, I thought we had the making of a really nice team. The now infamous reshoot, about which there was a great deal of gossip and not because the film tested badly. On the contrary, it tested wonderfully well, but at the moment when Bill says, "It sounds like fun" and we gallop off to leave the Nexus, when we arrived down at the planet, basically I said, "Okay, Captain, you go this way and I'll go that way" and we split up. Whereas, that's not what the fans wanted to see. They wanted to see the two captains shoulder to shoulder. That was the whole purpose of bringing them together and that's not how it was. So the reshoot was a very sensible action. I think it could have been even more of that buddy quality in the last part of the movie.

Q.

Does the association of *Star Trek* bother you one way or the other?

A.

It bothered me in anticipation. A lot. I spent a large part of the last four years working really hard to create for myself a career and identity that was apart from Captain Picard. For that reason I have spent Christmas for the last five years running my show [*A Christmas Carol*], which is coming back to Broadway. I wanted to let people know that I was a stage actor and I have a stage history. The kind of roles that I have had and the opportunities to accept have been few because *Star Trek* eats up so much of the year, but my role of the maitre'd from hell and the monstrous drug barren, and doing things like *The MGM Story* for Turner was a very important step, and then I did an action movie with Pierce Brosnan. All of this was very calculated because I did have genuine fears that the role might become an albatross around my neck. I hope I have a lot of working life ahead of me and I didn't want to find a handicap. So far as I can see, it has on the contrary opened up all kinds interesting and exciting possibilities for me. This summer I was in New York filming a stage play, *Jeffrey*, in which I played the middle-aged gay lover of a young man who was a dancer and HIV positive. It was simply a grand experience not only because the script was truly brilliant, but it gave me the opportunity to play a character who was just about as different from Picard as you could find; an outrageous, ironic flamboyant individual who believed the best way to deal with AIDS was to laugh at it but who has a tragic story because, of course, his lover dies at the end of the movie. Right now I am shooting a movie called *Let it Be Me*, which is a romantic comedy set in a world of a ballroom dancing studio and I play a New York dancing coach who is a bit of a hustler as far as the women are concerned. I had the thrilling experience of not only acting with but also dancing with Leslie Carol, who is my partner. Four days ago she and I literally danced down 54th Street to the soundtrack of Frank Sinatra. I thought that that was probably a good moment to end my career. I didn't think it could get much better than that and, in fact, Leslie and I spent the whole Thursday and Friday dancing and the movie ends with our marriage, dancing the wedding waltz to Bing Crosby singing "True Love."

Q.

Did you have much training for that?

A.

I did. I came back to New York for almost two weeks of ballroom dance training and one of the nicest things about this movie is that people are paying me money to come in and learn to ballroom dance, and to spend my days with beautiful women in my arms. So, we foxtrot and quick step and I do a pretty smooth Waltz and my Tango is something to be seen. I do the Mambo, I have Cha-Cha steps. I even have a few little tap steps that I do with Elliot Gould.

Q.

Like *Dirty Dancing*.

A.

Of course, the film is written and directed by Eleanor Bernstein who wrote *Dirty Dancing*. So there is a certain amount of that in the movie too. In our wedding party there are some hip-hop dancers and there is also a guy who does break-dancing too,

and it's spectacular.

Q.

When you were that 17 year old kid mixing concrete, what was the dream like and how is the reality different from that dream?

A.

I never permitted myself dreams that would have encompassed the reality of today. When I was mixing cement, my dreams were exclusively fixed on being a Sheakespearean stage actor and it was all I wanted to be. Finally, in 1966, I was accepted into the Royal Shakespeare Company. I felt that there was nowhere else I would ever want to go. I was about as happy as I could possibly be and right at the end of that first season, they offered me a three year contract to stay on — I can picture right now the phone booth where I called my wife and said, "It has happened. I am just going to stay here forever." But that it should ever segue into an American TV series was something that I could not have imagined and there is nothing about it — not a single day — that I would have changed. I feel myself extraordinary blessed.

• • • •

Q.

Now, to kind of quote Malcolm McDowell and paraphrase, he said the RSC was not his cup of tea when he was there, but he was there with you for a year or so?

A.

For one year, my very first season in 1966. Malcolm was a spear-holder and I do mean a spear-holder. He did not have a line to speak. Well, that is the reality. I, on the other hand, did have a handful of lines and I also had some understudy but largely I was there to understudy the lead actors. I didn't know Malcolm too well in those days.

Q.

Shakespeare has been a big part of your life. Do you have any advice to young people who are totally turned off by it?

A.

Well, if they are totally turned off by it, I certainly wouldn't want to urge it on them, but if someone has to spend some time with Shakespeare, I would want them to try to

believe that there is no one key that will unlock its appeal, no one answer, no one solution. One of the reasons Shakespeare and his works have survived over 400 years is because he has a multitude of ideas he deals with and if one child could connect with Shakespeare in some way, no matter how absurd it might seem, it is valid. It is his connection and that is his way into Shakespeare. Whatever it might happen to be. What a teacher has to do is find a way in for the child and once that door has been opened, then it will continue to open wider and wider.

Q.

Rumors and *Star Trek* really seem to go together a lot. I was wondering what do you think of the whole process of constantly having every thing you say dissected, truthful or not, and in particular one question about the rumor that on the set of the show you were very particular about the Captain's chair and that it was not to be sat in by anybody but you. Is that true?

A.

Yes, it is true and I kind of blush to recall that. All of that

belongs to my pre-Americanization days. I really do believe I was something of a pompous asshole when I first started and I was fortunate enough to work with a group of people who I think liked me enough to not want me to go on being a pompous asshole. Most notably among them, Jonathan Frakes, and it is true. I did make a fuss in the beginning that nobody should be allowed to sit in the chair — I mean nobody, under any circumstances whatsoever and I got incensed at times when they would write in scenes that somebody would sit in the chair, "Okay, okay. Number One can have the bridge, but he stays in his own chair." Anyway, I hope happily all of those uncomfortable days are behind me. I do remember calling a company meeting — they will all remember this — somewhere during the first season and Denise Crosby was still on the show in those days. I felt that the set was much too undisciplined and that we should all exhibit more self-control and so — I mean could you imagine? I'm talking like that to other actors. What was I thinking? I remember Denise saying, "Come on, Patrick. You know, it is just fun" and I said, "We are not here to have fun!" Well, as it proved I happened to have just about the funniest time that I have had in my life for the last five or six years on the show. Like I said, that's all part of my Americanization.

Q.

What broke the dam? What unleashed ....

A.

They wore me down. They wouldn't do the things I wanted them to do and they just laughed and made fun of me. Finally, I realized that it was all together much more comfortable just enjoying them and I would like to think that I actually became one of the most rowdiest, most disruptive characters on the show before the series was over.

Q.

What about you getting dissected by the fans and media? Did you ever feel like saying to the fans, "Get a life?"

A.

No, I never felt that. That has never been my view of the fans. Sometimes I think they are a little overly obsessed with the series and I cannot get that obsessed with it. Like when

people say to me, "Mr. Stewart, can you tell me exactly how fast is warp speed?" I say, "You couldn't get on the freeway" and I don't pour over the details where many of them do. It was for me at the beginning a job, although a job I took too seriously and I think that one of the strengths of the series finally was that all of us worked very hard but insisted on being as lighthearted as possible for as much of the time as possible. I think that became something infectious that passed through the group and I can see it in the movie, although some of my colleagues were disappointed to find that they didn't have more to do in the movie. And I was disappointed for them. Every single one of the people that I worked with are certainly fine actors and any one of them could lead one of the films. They have done it time and time again in the series. I was saying this to one of them the other night. It doesn't amount to the length of screen time that you get, but the quality of the screen time and every single moment one of my colleagues were on screen, was absolutely tremendous. There is a wonderful moment when Gates is seen through Geordi's visor and she was bending over him. If you have ever seen a more beautiful image than that on the screen, I can't image

where it is. It was just dazzling how Gates looks in that film. I think it is because of this continual feeling of good fellowship that we had on the show, that the cast was just as substantial as it really is.

Q.

Are you still married and do you have children?

A.

No, I am no longer married, but I do still have children. I have a son and a daughter. My son is an actor and my daughter is in the process of becoming an independent businesswoman.

Q.

How do you feel about one of your children being an actor?

A.

I was very uneasy about it in the beginning. Most actors are when their children say they want to be in the business, but he convinced me that he had to do it and I have no arguments against that. He is a good actor. He is a wonderful comedy actor.

Q.

Screen or stage?

A.

Well, his work has mostly been on the stage and that's where I enjoyed him most. He did make one appearance in an episode of *Star Trek* in a quite famous episode called "Inner Light," one of the best stories ever filmed, in which he played my son.

Q.

What's his name?

A.

Danny.

Q.

Could you talk a bit about your relationship with Shatner contrary to rumors that have been on the media lately?

A.

Yeah, that's right. But you know, who wants to write articles about how Patrick Stewart and Bill Shatner get along?

Who cares?

Q.

I do actually.

A.

Alright, then let's talk about it.

Q.

I mean you've got so much in common.

A.

Yeah, it is extraordinary how much in common we do have.

Q.

Was there any trepidation about meeting him?

A.

Bill has a bit of a brutal reputation that proceeds him, particularly in his relationship with his colleagues and I was uneasy about that. Also, there were stories that Bill had made certain negative remarks about our show in the early days, with him not being supportive. I've got to take that

up with him one of these days. But when we finally sat down together, he and I, it was a very productive. We were at the ShoWest convention in Las Vegas late one night and I had an early morning call the next day. The Paramount plane was put at my disposal and Bill said, "Can I get a lift?" So he and I flew back from Las Vegas together in the executive jet, just the two of us alone up in the sky for an hour and it was perfect because it gave us the opportunity to sit down and talk. We didn't talk about career. We certainly didn't talk about *Star Trek*. We talked about very personal things and it was the foundation to help us to work so well together when the movie began. He has become a good friend.

• • • •
BRENT SPINER
(Lt. Commander Data)

Q.

So, you clearly had no fun at all.

A.

Yeah, really. It was like dying and going to heaven, you know. I had been sort of euphemistically painting on a very narrow pallet for a long time with kind of muted colors, so it was a real opportunity to cut loose. When I first read the script, I was a little concerned about it just because it was so different even though it represented an evolution for the character, but in thinking about it, I finally came to the conclusion that in worse case scenario, they would love me in France.

Q.

Where does the character go from here now that it has achieved its goal?

A.

I think if I had my way about it

— which I hardly ever have — to me it seems that the character went from being child-like and naive in the series to being a different kind of child in this one because of the newness of the emotions and the inability to control them and know exactly how to handle them. He was a child with emotion and I think the obvious place to take the character is into a gradual maturity. An emotional maturity and that can only mean romance, can't it? I would hope that that is what would occur — a deepening or understanding of emotion and the subtleties, and how to deal with that is where it is going to go.

Q.

Where he went in the final episode, which of course, is one possibility....I kind of liked the fact that he became somewhat obnoxious.

A.

Yeah, me too.

Q.

It was somewhat of a logical progression.

A.

Yeah, it really was. When I read the final episode, I was thrilled to find that he became a professor at Cambridge and he was holding the same chair now as his old friend Steven Hawkings once did because we are very close, you know. I call him "The Hawk" actually. But, yeah, I thought that was a real logical place for him to go.

Q.

How much of Brent Spiner was now in Data?

A.

Well, certainly more, although I am not quite that immature emotionally — close, but yeah, there was more of me in it because I was able to use more of me. Initially, the beauty of a character like Data is that nobody can tell you that you are doing it wrong. There is no sort of standard for how an android behaves. So, I had that luxury for a long time but the movie required me to actually use more of myself.

Q.

What do you think is unique

about William Shatner and why do you think William Shatner has been so everlasting?

A.

You know, I'm not sure I can speak on the uniqueness of the character or Bill — I call him Bill, to let you know how close we are — but I think it is more — and this is just my opinion — what's the word — he is the quintessential hero. It's not a uniqueness at all. It may be just the opposite. It is something we all know and recognize and want to be and in sort of mythological terms, he is the hero who goes out in search of something to bring back to his people, which is the essence of all mythology and be it a weapon or intelligence or medicine or whatever, the hero goes out in search. I think Bill had sort of embodied that mythological hero. It's something that we all respond to.

Q.

How would you contrast that with Patrick's captain?

A.

Patrick's captain — it is taking that same hero and applying to it civilization and the ability to negotiate rather than use force, and I think Patrick projects just wisdom and intelligence and I think that time has evolved the idea of a captain.

Q.

Do you call him Pat?

A.

I sometimes do just to irritate him.

Q.

Obviously you worked with David Carson on the series — what's his approach? Has his approach changed at all from doing an episode to doing this multi-million dollar movie?

A.

Well, his approach wasn't necessarily different except that he had the luxury of more time. Generally on the series we were shooting between eight and ten pages a day. On the feature we were doing between two and three pages a day. So, that afforded both David and the cast the opportunity to try more and to actually get it right as opposed to just get it. As a director in general — and I was

more aware of it on the film because I actually, in the episodes David has directed, never had that much to do. One episode I had a bit, but I worked with him more on the film than I had prior to that. I found him really, really bright, prepared and whenever I would be at a loss of where to take something, he had a real clear vision on where it should go. I found him enormously helpful and I admired his sort of digging his heels in because as always happens, I think there are time constraints and there are monetary constraints that the studio has to be concerned about. But David made his primary concern, I think, to make a good picture and just basically refused to be budged on that notion.

Q.

They wanted him to cut the ocean scene.

A.

The boat scene?

Q.

The boat scene. He told me that was the first thing they wanted him to cut.

A.

Before we started shooting, yeah, but again he would basically just dig his heels in and say, "I don't want to just make a movie, I would like to make a very good movie if possible" and he stuck to that all the way through the final day of shooting.

Q.

For you what was the difference between doing the series and the movie?

A.

Well, we had much better accommodations for one thing. It really was in the area of getting more takes and being able to just sort of go with an instinct and try it and take things to extremes that we weren't able to do in the series. Generally, in the series if you say your lines right and you hit your mark, that's good enough. Performance really isn't a factor too often and in the feature, we had the opportunity to do more takes and go into a different direction and try this and that. It was just a more creative sort of thing for an actor, which you like to do anyway. That was basically

the difference for me and the way the character evolved was different for me as well.

Q.

Was a collaborative process going on as the character evolved during the filming in terms of the script? Did you bring anything to it — as you were saying bringing your own personality and emotions to it, any lines, working with the writers or the director?

A.

Yeah. Actually we had a lot more input into the film than we usually did in the series. That again was because of time restraints. On the series, we would be finishing an episode at midnight or 2:00 a.m. and starting another one the next day and barely had time to read it, much less really address the problems that we had. We just had to do it. In this case, I had several meetings with the writers and with Rick and David and was able to give notes on it and make adjustments to it and there was more freedom on the set. I could actually ad lib an odd moment or two, which was rarely done in the series, because again of time and in this case we were able to say, "Sure, you can try one like that."

Q.

Do you remember your ad libs?

A.

There are a couple. Most of the ab libs for me happened in the laughing sequence. The whole thing with using the tricorder as the puppet and Mr. Tricorder and doing an imitation of Patrick and things like that. I also got to make up the little tune that I did later

Q.

You made a few major moves in your life. Were those hard decisions to make? Were they difficult times?

A.

Well, the move to New York — I was quite young and I had just got out of college and that was difficult because I came from Texas and I had never heard of Long Johns, for example. I didn't know what they were. I literally thought I was going to die the first year I came to New York just from the cold. I had no idea and I didn't know how people lived here. It was so cold and then somebody told me about those magic things called Long Johns, but, yeah, I came from a suburban neighborhood in Houston, Texas and it couldn't be any more different from living in an urban city, particularly New York City. So, it took me a couple of years of living here before I really adjusted to it and, you know, when that happens it is like suddenly there is no other place on earth to live other than New York, but I was here for eleven years. I did a lot of theatre, did around 25 plays, and became very broke as happens, and figured that I got too old to do what I was doing and I needed to start sort of living my life as an adult and that kind of required actually making an income. So, I went to LA. Actually I went to LA with *Little Shop of Horrors*.

Q.

Now, was that a difficult decision? I mean to grow up?

A.

You know, I still haven't committed to it entirely but sure, you know, it was actually because I really enjoyed that sort of Bohemian — being a struggling artist. That had a very romantic notion to me as a child. I thought that was the way you were supposed to do it

and I still kind of believe that. When I came to New York, there was no option really. If one was serious about being an actor, you came to New York and you did theatre and you struggled and that was just part of the deal and there is hardly anything better when you are young, really. It was ideal.

Q.

How did you find LA?

A.

Well, that was the reward finally. I got to warm up and I was used to a mobile community. Houston is very much like LA. It is sort of like a dress rehearsal for LA. It's probably never going to open, but they are similar towns actually just in terms of what they feel like. It wasn't much of an adjustment really.

Q.

A lot of your co-stars were resigned to the fact that they weren't going to have a lot of screen time in this movie. That wasn't a problem with you, but I'm just wondering whether or not — you know, because you seem to be a pretty close cast, did that put any sort of pressure? Actors are actors.

A.

That's true. It was not derisive among us. It really —there was nobody who was upset with anybody else as far as the cast is concerned with the size of our roles. I think those in the picture who have the larger roles — as you say, actors are actors and even the ones of us who had larger roles didn't feel we had enough. So, no one ever does, you know. So, no, it didn't cause any friction between the cast.

Q.

So, what about since the end of filming, did it really hit you that the series is over and have you had much interaction with the rest of the cast?

A.

Yeah. We still speak every week, most of us, and we are sort of connected. We really became — I know this is really boring — I wish I could give you some dirt here. I really do. If you like, I will make something up, but we got along famously. Making a TV series is hardly adverse conditions, but we were on sound stages in uncomfortable make-up for 15 to 18 hour days, almost every day for seven years and if we didn't hate each other after that, it just was never going to happen. We actually got on very well through the entire run. I can't imagine many jobs better than the one we had for the simple reason that what kind of job is it that you get to go to work every day with your friends and laugh all day long? That's basically what we did and as a result we are still incredibly close. I mean, I had been with Patrick last week. I was best man at LeVar's wedding and so I speak with LeVar all the time and I spoke to Marina last night. We keep in really close contact.

Q.

Were you ready to move on? Most of you had signed for an eighth season I understand, and then Paramount decided to forget the show and do the movie. Some of the actors — and I think Patrick was one of them — were ready to move on. He said, "We have done this for seven years. I'm done." Are you one of those people who were ready to move on?

A.

Yeah. We had done 178 hours. One hundred and seventy eight hours of anything is just about enough, I think. It was a brutal

sort of seven years of work and I was glad not to have to get up at 5:00 in the morning any more. I think we were really almost all ready to stop doing it. Maybe a couple of people would have been interested in doing an eighth season, but not many of us really. I think we felt, "Yeah, we have done this now for seven years and with luck, we will get to come back and do it every couple of years."

Q.

The movies would still be interesting to you?

A.

Yeah, well, again for the reason that I get to come back together with my friends and have some fun. It would be like going to summer camp every couple of years.

Q.

Is that the plan for your character, basically to come back in the next movie or perhaps another one? Or any other plans?

A.

You know what? I don't know

if there are any plans. I think it is sort of an economical factor and I think that is the bottom line on it. If the movie does well, undoubtedly, I think the studio would like to make another one and if it doesn't do well, than we probably won't.

Q.

Do you have a favorite scene in the movie?

A.

To be completely honest, I haven't seen the whole movie. I just did looping and consequently I only looked at myself. So, at this point in time I am my favorite thing in the movie, but I haven't seen it yet. So, I may change my mind once I have seen it.

Q.

What's next?

A.

I am just sort of crossing my fingers and hoping for the best because I don't know. Having been associated with a project that I consider a quality project for this length of time, I am reluctant to just jump into anything else. I also feel that I had the good fortune of having a really sweet character to play for a long time and I'm not that eager to do something where I get to say, "This is really me." If I had my choice, it would be another extreme character of some sort, but I think it remains to be seen whether my identification with the role is going to be detrimental in terms of the rest of my career. At the moment, I don't feel particularly any more typecast than say Harpo Marx.

Q.

Have casting directors typecast you?

A.

Do you know what is interesting, I am finding — and I think this is true — that *Star Trek* is not really an industry show. It is not like, say, *NYPD Blue* or *Seinfeld* or something that the industry watches. They are aware of it. They know it is there. I find that when I go in to audition for things now, people don't actually know who I am and I see that as a benefit, actually. You know, that they don't have a perceived notion of who I am.

Q.

Can you talk a little bit about your makeup and also your eyes in this film in terms of what it required and what it is all about?

A.

Basically, it is gold powder that is put on about three inches deep and yellow contacts and I think, what I have seen of the film, is for the first time that it actually looks gold. People are who watch the series ask me, "Now, are you white or are you green?" and I was neither. I think depending on the quality of the television set — but it was always gold and in person when people would meet me on the set, they would always be startled by the color of it because it was not what they were used to seeing. Then again, that is part of the time constraint of a series. They were not able to light specifically for the color of my skin and John Alonzo who shot the picture is a master — beautiful — I mean he is a master. The first day that he saw me he went, "You're gold!"

Q.

Was the crying scene difficult to do? Did they have to redo it a couple of times to get it the right way?

A.

You know, I think we did it once, actually. Yeah. It was kind of like motor oil.

Q.

With all that makeup on, wasn't it difficult as far as your skin? Uncomfortable?

A.

It was not particularly uncomfortable and it didn't really cause problems with my skin because Paramount was kind enough to finance a facial for me every other weekend for fear that I would look like a teenager on screen. The only thing that was really difficult was the contacts. They were ordinary soft contact lenses — prescription contact lenses — they weren't my prescription, but they were prescription. The only real difficulty was that the makeup would get into my eyes and kind of smear over the contacts, so I couldn't really see very well about midway through the day. But that was all that was difficult.

Q.

You guys were always notoriously playing practical jokes on one another. Who was the most abusive cast member?

A.

But you know what? Oddly, we weren't really practical jokers. I had heard that before. I mean nobody put like buckets of water over the doors or anything. It was nothing like that. We were sort of — I actually think it was a cast of comedians and truly everyone was funny, and it was like a big night club act that would go on all day long and only be interrupted by having to do scenes from the show. So, I think — it was just again being inside 18 hours a day on sound stage. It necessitated levity and it was abundant.

Q.

What about guest shots on either *Deep Space Nine* or *Voyager*. Would you rule those out for the first year or —

A.

I wouldn't rule them out, but I might be more interested in doing them if I could play something else.

Q.

Has it been talked about?

A.

No. Well, other than just now?

Q.

I'll talk to Rick for you.

A.

Would you? I'm not particularly eager to do that. Not because of any negative feeling about those shows. It is just, again, I have done 178 hours of *Star Trek* television and if they desperately needed me, certainly I would come on and do it but I don't think that is the case and I don't desperately need to do that. I'm more interested right now in doing other things.

Q.

Do you watch *Deep Space*?

A.

No, but I didn't watch our show either. I watched the first two years of it and that was around 50 episodes and I thought, that's enough.

Q.

Deep Space Nine?

A.

Of our show. I got it. I enjoyed it. I figured actually that for the rest of my life it is going to be in re-runs and some day I am going to be in a hotel room in Shaboygen and I'm going to turn on the television and I would rather it be an episode that I hadn't seen before. So, I thought I am going to save five years of this for later.

Q.

I was reading through *Entertainment Weekly* and it talked about an album you have out or coming out?

A.

Well, it is already out actually. It has been out a couple of years.

Q.

Do you plan on doing any more?

A.

Yeah. I would like to do another album. I'm waiting until I'm really ready to lose a whole lot more money, because it was a total vanity production. and Wendy Nuss, who is one of the producers on the series, produced it. Dennis McCarthy did the arrangements for it. The guys on the show sang backup on one number with me and it was just something we wanted to do and we did and actually it is something that I am very proud of. I think it came out exactly as we wanted it to.

Q.

What's it called?

A.

It is called "Oh, Yellow Eyes is Back."

Q.

Have the Sunspots sang anything?

A.

The sunspots have not sung together, but I'm sure independently they have. That's what my backup group is called — The Sunspots.

Q.

Brent, are you married? Do you have children?

A.

No, I'm not and I don't.

Q.

How old are you?

A.

Let me think? Do you know what, let me just say this, when I turned 39, I realized what a genius Jack Benny really was.

Q.

Are you into computers and technology and all that stuff? I mean, how did you get the technobabble?

A.

Well, only because I'm an actor. I memorized it, exactly. I mean, the role actually required more memorization than anything else on the show. I think most actors would say this, but they like not to learn their lines, not to have them down pat when they come in, that it is through the rehearsal process and so on, but that was impossible with this because I was saying things that my mouth had never said before and it really was a matter of muscle learning. You couldn't just learn the lines in your head. They actually had to be spoken out loud before you got there or you were going to be in big trouble and we found that often with our guest stars who were unused to it. Their process was what they usually brought to something and this required a different sort of homework, but in general I am not particularly a technical person. I do have a computer but I am certainly not literate with it and often I hadn't a clue of what I was talking about. I really didn't. I found out, but I had no idea what it meant. The fans of the show understand it much better than I did.

Q.

Didn't the series provide you with some interesting acting opportunities?

A.

That's true. Initially my fear was when I got the part, that it was going to be a very limited part to play and it was anything but that. I wound up being — not only did the character have an arc in which he grew through the seven years towards humanity and understanding the subtleties and idiosyncracies of what it means to be a human, I also got to play a lot of other characters. Data trying on different forms of humanity like Sherlock Holmes and things like that. Then I also got to play my brother and my father at different ages and there are episodes where I would play four or five characters. It couldn't be a better part than that.

Q.

And that part is very rare where a character can progress that subtly.

A.

It truly is. I remember in the very beginning I had a meeting with Gene Roddenberry where we discussed where we wanted the character to go, both of us, and his notion, and I quite agreed with him, was the journey that my character would be on if the show progressed that far, was that with each passing year he would get closer and closer to humanity and finally would be extremely close but still not a human and I think that was the way it went and I think it is still going that way. I was delighted that in the film that it didn't just stop, that we actually had some movement in the character.

Q.

How did you get the role?

A.

I auditioned just like —

Q.

Were there lots and lots of people?

A.

There were quite a few people and finally it came down to me and one other guy and fortunately I think Tom Cruise decided he wanted to do films, so it fell to me.

Q.

Who is the movie going to appeal to? Is it just going to be *Star Trekkers* or does it have more of a universal appeal?

A.

I don't know. I hope it has a more universal appeal. I think if it is just an entertaining picture in general, I think it appeals to everybody. Certainly the Trekker has more insight into the subtleties of it, but I think it is just a cracking good action adventure movie. Hopefully that will appeal to a lot of people.

· · · ·
MALCOLM MCDOWELL
(Dr. Tolian Soran)

Q.

Malcolm, I thought it was just hilarious that here are two RSC guys duking it out in the California dessert.

A.

Right.

Q.

When you were at RSC, did you ever have any idea of the success you would achieve?

A.

Oh, I had a total premonition. No, of course not.

Q.

What was your dream?

A.

Certainly it wasn't to be duking it out with Patrick Stewart on top of some bloody mountain in the Valley of Fire, that's for sure, but I don't know. It is strange the way life comes into full circle, isn't it? So, I worked with Patrick when I was very young. He was somewhat younger. Although he looked just the same — bald. I always rather envied him in those days because he could play any part, you know, any age. He could play old men and did when he was in his twenties. I think he used to have this piece that he used to pop on for auditions but I think he was always more successful with the bald look.

Q.

And you worked with him in which production or show?

A.

I worked with him when I was on Stratford Upon Avon and I was there in 1965. Productions we did were *Henry IV Part I, Part II*. They were good sleeping pills. *Henry V* and various other productions and Patrick was a member of that company and so was I, but there were 100 actors in that company so it wasn't like we were buddies together. We weren't, but we knew each other and got on quite well.

Q.

When you were that kid, in having a dream that most actors have, how was the reality different from the dream?

A.

Well, my dream pretty much came true and I'm sure his did because soon after I left the Royal Shakespeare Company .... I hated it by the way. I loathed it. I thought it was like working for the damn government. It was no different. All the political crap that went on.

Q.

And you had to do all those plays.

A.

That was the only good part about it. It was just horrendous. I mean they rehearsed, the wastage, the boredom of it. I hated it. Obviously Patrick liked it. He was there for 12 years. I thought they should all get a medal for that.

Q.

How long were you there?

Best known for his roles in A Clockwork Orange *and* Time After Time, *Malcolm McDowell portrayed* Generations *villain Dr. Tolian Soran (photo copyright ©1995 Albert Ortega).*

A.

One year. That was enough for me. It was like being sentenced to Sing-Sing.

Q.

How did you leave the RSC?

A.

When I left the Royal Shakespeare Company I remember saying to Peter Hall, who ran the company — you have to go meet with him at the end of season and he would give you your marching orders or tell you what exciting things lay in prospect for you. So, six of us met in the pub, The Dirty Duck, and we were young revolutionaries if you like and troublemakers, agitators, you know, and we would say — I remember saying things like "This is all crap. I'm going in there. I'm going to tell this guy to stick this damn company — I feel like I am here just to move furniture," because that is basically what the young actors do. They come in, they bring on the crown or throne and then the actor comes in and sits on it and you stand by it and then you take the damn thing off. That is what drove me nuts.

Now, there were six of us, I remember saying, "We're going in there. We are going to tell this guy where to stick this damn company" and, of course, I was the first in and I did tell him, "There is no way. I don't care what you had in mind for me. I'm out of here. I'm gone. I'm history" and I'm going off. He said, "What are you going to do?" I said, "I'm going to be a movie star." Ha, ha, ha. Laugh, laugh, laugh. So, I'm waiting for the other five to come back to The Dirty Duck and they come in eventually and I said, "You told him?" "Well, he offered me the third duke from the right and you know, I think it could be a great part." "Twelve lines!" "Well, there are ways I could put a lot of emotion in —" I was the only one. I talked myself out of a job. But there you are. You take your chance and within, I think, a year I was starring in my first movie. So, I was very lucky.

Q.

Have there been many ups and downs?

A.

There have been so many. I think careers go up and down, up and down, up and down. I think what I have learned is in the down time when nobody seems to want you and you are in cold storage, you learned how to use that time productively and not get down on yourself. You have to be philosophical about it and you know it is a cross — from an actor's point of view, this profession is one of rejection. I don't even care if you are Tom Cruise. I mean, Anne Rice rejected him. Didn't want him. I don't care who you are, there is always that element of rejection and, of course, you have to have thick skin about it. I used to say, "Oh, well, they didn't want me to do that part. They are the losers, not me." But, of course, you know, that was a way of getting through it.

Q.

But what do you do?

A.

Oh, you get on with another life — you have another life. You have a family and another life entirely and I think that is important. The work is only the work, but the real life is what is really important.

Q.

Did you dislike Shakespeare or was it just the RSC?

A.

I think more the RSC. I think I am not a very good company member. That's why I could never do what Shatner and Stewart have done. I could never be a company man for seven years in the same part. It would drive me insane.

Q.

How do you feel about becoming part of the *Star Trek* phenomenon?

A.

I'm not going to be part of it. I'm onto the next thing already and that's it.

Q.

What is next?

A.

Well, I finished a movie called *Tank Girl,* which was a cartoon in Europe which is kind of a fun piece. So, it is a big budget thing for UA. We'll see how that goes.

Q.

How did this come about actually? When you were first approached — when you heard *Star Trek,* what went through your mind?

A.

Well, I had an open mind about it because, you know, I don't think I would do the series on television just because it doesn't appeal to me very much. I read the script and although I didn't really understand the script, I couldn't understand a word of it with all that Nexus stuff. I didn't know what the hell they were talking about but I thought there was a glimmer of a part there. A glimmer of some things that could be fun. So, they asked for a meeting and I went into a meeting with them and they asked me to read for it. I said, "No, I won't." It was ridiculous. What do they think it is, Shakespeare? So, I wouldn't read it but I had a very good meeting with Rick Berman and David Carson, and I think we got to talking about Patrick Stewart in the old days and there was a tape on. I hope he never sees this, but I think they said something about how old Patrick Stewart was and, of course, I knew how old but I am not going to tell today, but when they said at this meeting how old he was, I said "Yeah, that's right." So, we just had a bit of a laugh. Anyway, Rick Berman told me it was a very, very funny tape. So, I closed the door on the way out and they knew they wanted me to play the part.

Q.

So, did you have fun?

A.

Yes, I did. It was great because working with Patrick was fun for me because I knew him all those years ago and I have bumped into him at various times through our lives and I always liked Patrick, you know. What's not to like? He's a nice guy and I didn't really know what to expect when I worked with Bill Shatner, but he was a gentleman — very professional. We had all these fights and then we went back and shot the damn thing. It was a never ending ending.

Q.

I understand you were the one who announced you were killing Kirk.

A.

Yes, I was.

Q.

You let the word out early.

A.

Probably. Somebody asked me and I told them. And then I said, "Oh, did I do something wrong. Nobody told me not to say anything." They said, "No, it's okay." Well, yes, I shot him in the back originally and then I think they wanted him to have more of a heroic death. So, he fell off a bridge that I blew up. I suppose I would be held up on manslaughter rather than murder in the first. So, I think I am responsible for his death. It is just that I wasn't there to actually tread on his fingers and let him drop down that 200 foot cliff — but if they had asked me, I would have been there like a shot.

Q.

Malcolm, when Hollywood casts villains, why do they always cast the English actors?

A.

I think you should address that question to these idiots out there. I don't know. The English make good villains for some reason. Going back — way back. I remember talking to James Mason about that. I said, "Oh, you will be in that villain category and that will be it." But he had a very busy career. I don't mind — I love playing villains. I must say that it is nice to change occasionally, but I always have fun playing villains and I never take it too seriously, of course. I think villains are always the most interesting parts, usually, and what I like particularly about playing the villain is you don't have to be in every day. So, it's lovely. You don't have to carry the piece. The shoe leather as I call it. Being there for every shot. You just come in and steal the scenes that you are in and then you are on to the next.

Q.

Do you think this movie will make more younger people aware of who you are?

A.

Who knows? It depends on, I suppose, whether it is successful or not. If it is successful, I suppose it will, but I quite like the place that I am in. I rather like having people that know me because they have had to work at it a bit. I don't like to be too accessible through a TV show or something like that. It's much nicer and better where I am.

Q.

Do you think people still remember you from a lot of the earlier movies?

A.

Some do. Some do and then it is nice. They were wonderful films and I'm very, very happy that I did them, but life moves on. You can't dwell on the past.

Q.

Have you ever considered — I'm sure you must have — how *Clockwork Orange* nowadays is almost like a documentary?

A.

Yes, it is indeed. Well, of course, it is a brilliant film anyway. It is not so violent. I remember when it came out, I was actually shocked at the way the Americans particularly jumped on this whole thing of the violence of *Clockwork Orange*. I thought if they ever read the book, they would realize how much it was tamed down. Don't they ever read the newspapers? The violence is out in the street, you know. I think it is sort of an extraordinary message. Really, the film to me is not about the violence although, of course, that is very much a part of it, but it is really about the freedom of a man to choose what he wants to do and I think a sacred right of a human being is choice.

Q.

Wasn't that banned in Britain?

A.

It wasn't banned in Britain. There seems to be some confusion because Stanley Kubrick had the power to stop the film from being shown in Britain. I think he is rather paranoid about any gangs coming around and whacking him on the head or something. I don't know what his reason is for it, but I know it is not censorship. It is more Stanley. I think he is very paranoid about it. Maybe he's right. I don't know. I don't live in England any more.

Q.

Was Soran a particularly physical role for you?

A.

It was. It is not running the mile or anything or a marathon, but it was a fun role. I mean there is no question about it, I really enjoyed it. I enjoyed finding the character because it really wasn't on the page of the script. I really in my mind have this idea that this man was like a drug addict — had to get a fix and he wouldn't let anything divert him from that one goal. He was a very concentrated man. I really liked Soran as a character. I don't think he is a bad man at all. I've played much meaner. He is not a mean character. He has no malice really. Yes, he was going to destroy a planet with 230 million souls or whatever. But....you know.

Q.

I understand you really enjoyed the scenes with the Klingons.

A.

I loved those Klingons. Oh, those girls. They are just party girls, you know. Especially when they got their teeth out. But, of course, when I walked — when I came into a room and there they were, I would never recognize them in years. Boy, they were pretty well endowedm, let's put it that way. That is about all I was looking at the whole time. It is like working with two Patrick Stewarts.

Q.

Christmas is coming. What was your most memorable Christmas?

A.

Oh, my God. My most memorable Christmas? Oh, I think when I was a child. Of course, Christmas is for children really. Now, it is pretty ghastly. I think I remember it most as a child — opening the presents and being with the family.

Q.

Where?

A.

For me it was in Liverpool in England.

Q.

Were you poor? Were you rich?

A.

Middle class. Suffering middle class. It was just the same then as it is now. Although we weren't rich by any means, we never really suffered. We always did quite well.

Q.

Didn't you narrate the documentary, *The Compleat Beatles.*

A.

Yes, I did.

Q.

Was there any reason? I didn't realize the Liverpool background.

A.

Paul McCartney asked me to do it.

Q.

Did he really?

A.

He didn't ask me personally but I was on a Concord flight with him and Linda and it was soon after that I got a call saying would I do it. I said I would like to see it before I did it and I saw it and it was a brilliant film. Of course the Beatles are very much a part of my history, because one went in tandem with Beatles because they opened it up for the people of Northern England and they made it easier for me to be an actor, really. For sure. I have always been very fond of them. I veer more towards John Lennon probably than Paul McCartney. That's probably just the way I become think. Although one could admire Paul McCartney, I think the real heart of the group was John Lennon. But, of course, without either of them, they would never have been anything — because they were so competitive and I think that Paul McCartney was

so brilliant for John because he would come up with all these great tunes and then John would have to try and top him, and he was so lazy of course. Because if it hadn't been for McCartney, I don't think Lennon would ever have written anything, hardly. You know, it's true.

Q.

Of course, you have to throw George Martin in there somewhere too.

A.

Well, George Martin just mixed a good sound and just produced it. What has George Martin done since? The real true greatness is really those two — although the four of them actually. The way they came together was a whole era really. It was more than just four provincial lads. The stuff that they wrote really in retrospect is staggering. We are talking in terms of the greatest composers of this century — up there with them — the Gershwins and all that. They can hold their own with any of them. But I do believe it was all to do with uping one on each other and competition between them.

• • • •
WILLIAM SHATNER
(Captain James T. Kirk)

Q.

In your book, *Star Trek Movie Memories*, you make a big point of how difficult it was to gear up to play the death scene of Kirk. Then you had to go back and do it again. Was it easier the second time around?

A.

There are people in history who have died more than once —who have been resurrected and died again.

Q.

I've heard that.

A.

I'll play it straight. It took me some time to think about how I wanted to play the scene and to play it as honestly as I could. It required some self-examination — all that kind of thing. I could go into more detail, but I'll shorthand it. So, it was very emotional for me that first time we did it. And then, six weeks later when I was up in Toronto doing TekWar I got a call from the producer saying we have to go back and shoot it again. Malcolm's reaction, Patrick's reaction and my reaction apparently was the same. Was it my performance? And they said, "No." Somehow everybody lost sight of the fact that I was being shot in the back and it kind of slipped away — the whole ending kind of slipped away. They wanted more action and they were going to change the shot in the back, but the dialogue remained the same. So, yes, I had to go back and die again, but by this time I had worked out the performance, so I didn't need to look at it with the clarity of what's it like to die and what am I going to be like when I die and how frightened I am of dying and what would Captain Kirk do when he crosses that threshold. I had already done that. So, the second time I knew the performance. I had opened already.

Q.

Even though you did die, you are not necessarily dead or at least — or are you necessarily dead. I mean, logic would suggest that anything is possible. Is he really dead. Is the character out of the —

A.

Well, I understand the nature of your question having fooled you a couple of times before — not fooled you, but just people said, "Well, the movie made money, maybe we better bring you back to life" and stuff like that because we certainly meant it at the time, but in this case, there is a whole different cast and they want their time and place in the sun and our cast is — It would be impossible to bring the two casts together. We are separated by time and there is no logic in this in the way the story works.

Q.

When did logic have that much to do with it?

A.

When did logic have that much to do with it? Well, there is an internal logic. A theatrical logic.

Q.

Bill, are you a workaholic?

• • • •

From Trek to Tek: Wiliam Shatner with Greg Evigan, star of TekWar, the USA cable series based on Shatner's best selling novels (photo copyright ©1994 MCA TV).

A.

Am I a workaholic?

Q.

In your lifetime you have done more things than any of us could ever dream of ever doing.

A.

From my point of view, I'm grasping opportunities because you never know when it all might stop. No, I don't think of myself as a workaholic, although I heard the word attached to me this year. As you see, I have *Star Trek Movie Memories* and *TekPower* and *TekWars*, which debuts January 7th on the USA Network, and CBS has *Rescue 911*, the miracle show that saved 300 lives and there is a special on CBS in November — the end of November. Then there is a conference call. Patrick Stewart and I are on a conference call with 4,000 other people. It has never been done before. It is a unique event.

Q.

When is that?

A.

December 11th at 6:00 in this time zone 4,000 people will be on the phone with Patrick Stewart and me. Then in the Central and Pacific time zones it will be repeated. So there will be a total of 12,000 people that will be either talking to Patrick Stewart or me. An operator will randomly select the people to ask the questions. It has never been done before. It is a unique telephone event.

Q.

How do they do that?

A.

By buying a card which would become a collectible and again in shorthand 1-800-TEC-TREK will give you all the information. So, I am enumerating the things I am involved with right now. There are many other things that are further down the line.

Q.

Radio and television? What are you talking about?

A.

I'm talking about picking up the telephone and dialing a PIN number — Personal Identification Number. You become part of 4,000 people all on the line at the same time. Is that astonishing to you?

Q.

It's out of *Star Trek*.

A.

It's out of *Star Trek*. Four thousand people will all be communicating at the same time. Now, they won't be able to speak all at the same time but they will all be listening to the hems and the haw. It will be live. We will be talking to you on the phone except all of us there and times a hundred — I mean, it is astonishing. That is what's happening. So, when something like that occurs to me it is not "I've got to keep working. I've got to keep working." To me, it's "My God!" In Toronto, there is a firm called CORE — it is a special effects house — that asked me when they formed their company, to be part of the company. I'm working in special effects. I work with digital computer effects.

TekWar is that. It seemed to be a natural evolvement to become part of that company. It seems to be natural for me to be part of a company that makes a future call. It is called The Future Call Company that does this. That has pre-paid telephone cards called TEC cards that not only can you make a long distance call from the card, but you have another 800 number that you can use to access a pre-program hour of entertainment in which many of the actors in *Generations* have a pre-recorded voice that I have interviewed. They are on tape. You can learn to speak Klingon if you press the right number. There is a whole thing. There is a burgeoning electronic envelope of entertainment that is taking place now and for me not to say, "God, I've got to be part of that" seems to be idiotic if I am offered the opportunity either by celebrity or by intelligence or by opportunity or having invented it.

Q.

But what about a life?

A.

But that is life. I'm having great fun telling you about that and seeing your eyes look up and say "Oh, God." That to me is part of my life. Now, my other part of my life is next week I go to Kansas City and compete in a horse show. I'm going to have dinner with my family on Sunday when I get back. I've got my life but all these things are —I mean, God, that's incredible.

Q.

But time runs out for all of us.

A.

But is time going to run out any sooner or slower if I don't do this and, in fact, people who slow down — people who retire — to use that word — die. But to me, I'm more alive and more sensual in the full meaning of that word — aware of my senses now than I ever have been because of all the things that are going on.

Q.

Are there still hard times?

A.

There are always hard times. Times are hard all the time.

Q.

People seem to want you and Patrick not to get along. I think the opposite is true. Truth is, I love him. He's a great guy. He has become a friend and in the short time that we have known each other, there is a bond that will last a lifetime and we'll work together again because we so enjoyed working together. He is a wonderful actor. He is a giving, kind and generous man. I can't say enough things kind about him and I admire him. But what amazes me is that — and I understand an editor saying, "Well, we've got to sell papers. Let's do what we can about selling Stewart and Shatner not getting along together." But, why would somebody think that to say they fought on the stage, didn't like each other, sell papers any more than these two guys met and love each other — the Shakespeare thing, the English and Canadian thing? That's just as newsworthy. That sells — to me — just as many papers. Maybe the tabloids are just evil and can't think in humane and human ways. I don't understand it. That to me is the most disturbing thing. That they think by saying something mean and actually lying, are they a newspaper? Do we consider them — the tabloids

— a newspaper? I'm asking that sincerely. Do we read them for some news because of that and we know most other things are absolutely inventions of somebody sitting at a typewriter and saying, "What will I invent today?" It has nothing to do with anything that is really happening. If they made a phone call to somebody on the set and asked, "So, how are they getting along?", they would have been told the truth. And then they could have embellished the truth.

Q.

We in journalism like to make the distinction, but I think unfortunately a lot of the reading public don't make that distinction that there are different types of newspapers.

A.

I understand, but I'm thinking the people — either the editor or the reporters sitting by the typewriter or the guy giving them their assignment, what do they think? Go invent something that is hateful. Why would they want to do that? It's the worst of the human spirit, and I find that disturbing. I like to think of people basically kind and by circum-

stances being mean as a necessity — "I want to eat my bread and you've got bread and I'll take that bread." I can understand that, but a guy sitting behind a desk saying, "Let's say they hate each other. It's better that way."

Q.

There have been some nasty things said about you by some of your costars.

A.

Well, even that I can understand. I can understand George Takei saying — "He comes up to me and says 'God, George, you look great' and he doesn't really mean it." I can understand him thinking he doesn't really mean it because he doesn't have the confidence in himself that he really does look great. I mean he really looks great. I heard this on the air. Somebody played a cut for me on the *Howard Stern Show*. George said, "He's the kind of guy who comes up and says you look great but he really doesn't mean it." I really mean it! He looks great! But, if he can't accept a compliment, well, that's his problem, but even that I can understand.

Q.

You are sort of in a unique position, I think, of being an actor who has taken a character and played it through nearly every stage of his adult life. I mean, have you given any consideration at all ?

A.

There is certainly the aging process. As the years went by, sure.

Q.

But nobody ever really had that opportunity I think.

A.

I guess not.

Q.

To play something literally through the years of his life.

A.

Yeah.

• • • •

Q.

Do you remember your first role?

A.

Yes, I remember it. Absolutely. I was in up — Montreal has the equivalent of the Catskill and I was on a farmin the mountains Mountains which had a camp for a number of children — it was part farm, part summer camp and the summer camp put on a play and that Sunday all the parents came to see the summer play and I was playing whatever it was I was playing. I made them cry and there was applause afterwards. This little kid that was six years old, loved it. You know how your memory is selective and you can forget what you did yesterday and certainly last year and ten years ago never happened, but to remember something when you six must have left an impression.

Q.

Has playing Kirk ever had a negative impact on your life at all in the sense of wherever you go ....

A.

A negative?

Q.

Yeah.

A.

No. I accept worshippers. Yes, you mean, does it put a distance between me and other people? I attempt to overcome it by lowering myself....

Q.

With the reaction the audience has had to your character's death, is it gratifying to know that?

A.

Yes. It is extraordinary playing a character over 30 years and, of course, it has been intermittent. It hasn't been a thirty year period for me. After three years of making the series and then ten years go by and then a movie and then a couple of months — two or three months — and then it disappears for another two or three years. It is very intermittent, although

the *Star Trek* comet trails behind us. But to have people think of the character as an entity and to mourn the death as though it was a real person, yeah, it's really gratifying.

Q.

Did you lose anything in having to reshoot the ending?

A.

No, no, no. The same dialogue is there. I hesitate to repeat myself because I wrote very carefully in the last chapter of this book, but again to give you shorthand of what is there. I find the death scene — you can only play, you can only perform, you can only read the lines as a result of your own experiences. I can't read a laugh line or a line of love the way you would because I don't have your experience of it, I only have my own. So, my coloring of a line is based on my experience. So, playing the death scene required me to look at what I would feel like if I were to die and we all avoid looking at our death. We all wear rose colored glasses, not on life so much but on the absolute certainty that you are going to die, and if it is not this instance in terms of time and for all intents and purposes your life is meaningless, because you have lived and died and who remembers? You understand what I'm saying. So, all those thoughts that we avoid completely and only in the most distressful moments do we think of, and then avoid thinking about them again until the next distressful moment, I had to think about because I wanted to play the death of the character as honestly as I could. So, I required myself to look at what I would feel like if I was to die and how I would like to die and what it was like to die. So I put that all together and played that the first time. The first time it was shot and what was changed in the second time was not being shot in the back, the mountain blowing up and the bridge, but the heart of the scene was not changed.

Q.

The captains are really a product of the times.

A.

Well, I keep hearing that and I'm sure that scholars of drama point to the fact that the drama of the era reflects the era, comedies and Shakespeare and musicals and the kitchen dramas of live television. But there is also a universal thread that goes through all drama, and that is the hero has an antagonist — the protagonist has an antagonist and there is action, there is plot and character movement and all those things that have been around since the Greeks wrote dramas. That's what I think makes an action hero, who is placed at the horns of a dilemma, and has his group of people around him who help and that makes the drama, as well as the decisions that they are allowed to make. I don't see that being a reflection of the violence of the late 60's.

Q.

There is a different situation on *Next Generation* — How would you characterize it?

A.

Yes, there is. Well, I would characterize it that in the beginning of the *Next Generation*, Roddenberry said in 300 years human beings will not be in conflict and the writers had to get around that.

Q.

Which is difficult to do.

A.

That's why so many writers came and went. They had to take a more philosophical route and make an internal conflict.

William Shatner reprised his role of Captain James T. Kirk one last time in Star Trek: Generations (photo copyright ©1995 Albert Ortega).

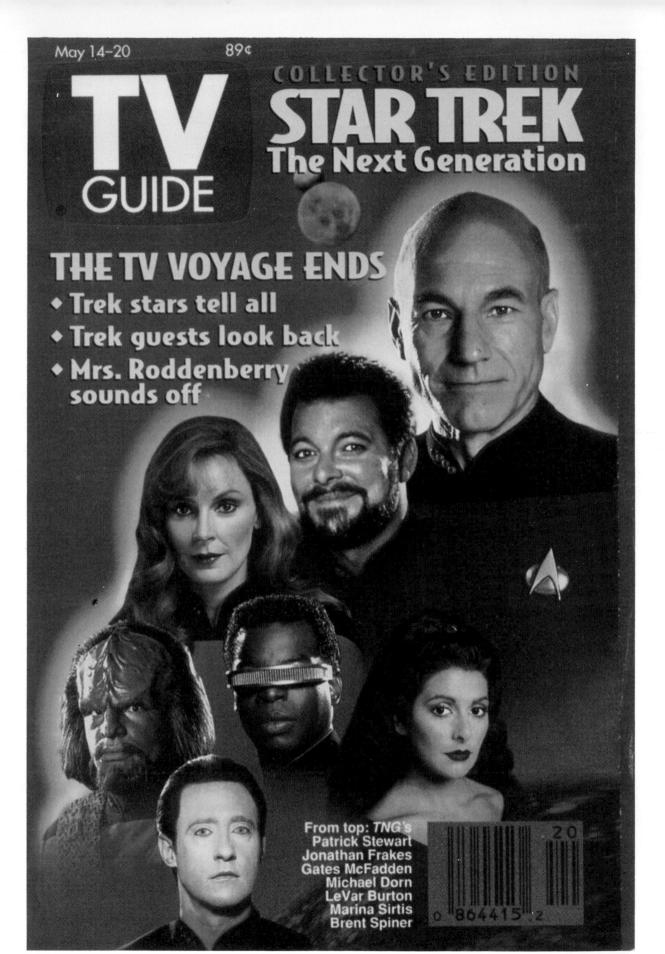

May 14–20   89¢

TV GUIDE

COLLECTOR'S EDITION
STAR TREK
The Next Generation

THE TV VOYAGE ENDS
- Trek stars tell all
- Trek guests look back
- Mrs. Roddenberry sounds off

From top: *TNG*'s
Patrick Stewart
Jonathan Frakes
Gates McFadden
Michael Dorn
LeVar Burton
Marina Sirtis
Brent Spiner

20

0 864415 z

● ● ● ●

APPENDIX A:
The Final Trek

Certainly, the final episode of *Star Trek: The Next Generation* proves that all good things truly do come to an end. Aptly titled, the final mission, "All Good Things" is a two-hour capper to seven years of intergalactic adventures. And while it proves a fitting end to the small screen voyages of the starship Enterprise, "All Good Things" certainly doesn't provide a coda — not with the legendary starship making its continuing voyages on the silver screen.

Nonetheless, the final episode of *Next Generation*, written by veteran *Trek* scribes Brannon Braga and Ronald D. Moore, is a more than satisfying finale in the tradition of such long-running shows as *M*A*S*H* and *Cheers*. Says Moore, "It's clearly an episode designed for people who know the series. They'll enjoy it and the layers of meaning and the way the characters have developed. They'll get a kick out of it."

Standing on the set on Stage 16 of Paramount Studios where a new starship bridge has been built for one of the finale's pivotal scenes, I think back to first setting foot on the set of *Next Generation* seven years ago, as a die-hard classic *Trek* fan who, like many others, was dubious of the potential for success of a new small screen *Trek*. Nonetheless, the sets were impressive, the cast engaging and the producers passionate. The ingredients were there to recapture the essence of what made the original *Star Trek* a cultural phenomenon — and yet it seemed hard to believe that a new show could transcend the die-hard cult of Trekkers and penetrate the mainstream of American television viewers who thought of fans as overweight, pimply kids who chanted "I Grok Spock" as a mantra and needed to "get a life."

Now, many of those same naysayers are converts. In its seven years on the air, *Star Trek: The Next Generation* has continually grown more and more popular, making it a $2 billion industry and a staple of most viewers' television diet. Much of the series' success is attributable to executive producer Rick Berman, a former television executive, who helped shaped the franchise by combining Gene Roddenberry's optimistic view of the future with strong storytelling, impeccable production values and assembling a winning creative team. Sharing in the Peabody Award and Emmy-winning success are executive producers Michael Piller and Jeri Taylor, who brought their own diverse experiences working on a myriad of mainstream television shows to the table.

Meanwhile, in the wake of the series' tumultuous early seasons, a solid writing team of young talent was nurtured — including a *Trek* fan turned writer, Ron Moore; a writing intern who became one of the show's most inventive producers, Brannon Braga; and a waiter and playwright who served as the show's story editor in its final seasons, Rene Echevarria, who also wrote third season's "The Offspring," considered by many of the show's cast to be *TNG*'s finest episode.

And here the weekly adventures of the 1701-D end, a climactic adventure which brings the Enterprise crew back to the beginning; both figuratively and literally. In the finale, originally entitled "Verdict," Picard finds himself back at Farpoint as Q presides in casting judgment over humanity.

"I enjoyed writing for Q again," says Ron Moore, who also penned `Tapestry,' one of the show's most popular episodes. "It's an interesting character in our pantheon." Moore also had the chance to write for Tasha Yar again in the finale's Farpoint sequences. "Tasha and I and Sela are old

● ● ● ●

friends," he laughs. "I've helped Denise Crosby and her career for a while now."

Coming up with a story that would fulfill expectations for the show's eagerly anticipated final episode was not a simple task, admits Moore. "It wasn't easy. It took a lot of effort and the toughest thing was getting approval on the story. Everyone wanted the story to be very special and there was a good week where we were trying to get the story approved and trying to get the story together. We were eager to get to the teleplay because we knew time was running out."

Equally challenging was writing the final scene which ultimately left the greatest lasting impressions on viewers. Few will forget the final scene of *Cheers* in which Sam Malone stands in his darkened Boston bar, straightens a crooked picture and turns off the lights forever. Similarly, Moore and Braga had the novel idea of revisiting a familiar staple of the show, the poker game. "We wanted it to be something sweet and sentimental and we wanted the whole family there together and we did not want to do it on the bridge," says Moore. "We thought it was the most obvious thing to do. It's kind of cold and its not very personal. We wanted to do one last poker game and end it there

with the whole family in a quiet, intimate setting. It seems like the crew at their best, sitting around and interacting."

The cast is cognizant of the significance of the final days of filming after a successful seven year run. They have become a tight-knit family of friends, and while there is some melancholy over the fact that divergent career paths will keep them apart, they know that bi-annual movies will reunite them on-screen and on-set. In addition, television reruns will lead to an assured broadcast immortality few actors ever experience.

Standing in old-age make-up to film some of the "All Good Things" key sequences, which take place 30 years in the future, Jonathan Frakes comments of *Next Generation*, "It's a show that I've been very proud to have been part of."

TV GUIDE takes you to the set of *Star Trek: The Next Generation* for the sci-fi series' finale on the Final Frontier—and brings you the parting thoughts of Patrick Stewart (below) and the entire cast as they look back with tears and laughter on seven seasons of starship voyages. In addition, there's a behind-the-scenes look at *Star Trek* secrets, talks with *Trek* guest stars, and an appreciation by author Ursula K. Le Guin.

NEXT WEEK
IN TV GUIDE

• • • •
APPENDIX B.
"Saturday Night Stewart"

Patrick Stewart recently appeared in a highly-rated installment of the popular variety show, *Saturday Night Live*. During the episode, he performed in several skits including as Captain Picard of the Love Boat Enterprise in which the cruise ship played host to a love-struck Ferengi (played by Al Franken), Charro and David Brenner. Bernie Koppel even put in a cameo appearance in the skit which featured Chris Farley as Riker and Rob Schneider as Data.

"I had a wonderful time doing it," says Patrick Stewart, who auctioned off the Enterprise/Love Boat at a recent Creation Convention. "It was exhausting, exhilarating and absolutely terrifying, and I would have not missed a moment of it for all the world. I love being in New York and they said they would invite me back."

Interestingly, during the show's rebroadcast in August 1994, *SNL* re-edited the episode, moving the *Star Trek* skit to its teaser and editing in footage from the dress rehearsal to replace some technical glitches made in the

Issue #7
$5.95

Epi-log Journal

The Television Journal of Science Fiction, Fantasy, and Adventure

March -April 1993

Gene Roddenberry Tribute Issue!
Part Three: *Star Trek* Animated * *Star Trek: The Next Generation*
PLUS extensive coverage of tv's scariest show: THE OUTER LIMITS!

original live telecast. In addition, the show's laugh track was sweetened. "That's what happens when you have a giant [Stewart] standing among pygmies," Brent Spiner told a convention crowd. "If everyone had been as good as Patrick it would have been a good show."

• • • •

....

APPENDIX C.
"Breast Of Both Worlds"

Troi's closet of low-cut outfits keep the cosmos safe for Cosmo. "If you go back to `Encounter At Farpoint' where I was dressed in the cosmic cheerleader outfit with the ugliest go-go boots ever designed, I was about 20 pounds heavier than I am now," laughs Marina Sirtis of the first in what would become one of her many outfits over the years. "Imagine a potato with matchsticks sticking out of it, and that was my shape. After the first episode, they decided the outfit didn't suit Troi's character because she was cerebral and kind of elegant. They decided they would design something more flattering, so they came out with the ugly gray spacesuit and they put a belt in a lighter colored fabric exactly where my fat was."

Unfortunately, according to Sirtis, the sexier her costumes got, the stupider her character became. "What happens is if the girls have cleavage, they cannot have a brain because the two don't go together. So when I got the gray spacesuit and got cleavage, she lost her brain matter. That was a shame because —

originally — Troi was not supposed to be the chick on the show. Gene [Roddenberry] said she was intended to be the brain on the show, which you would never know from watching it. She was supposed to have equal the intelligence of Spock."

Also found in Troi's closet in later years were a maroon jumpsuit and a green dress. "I lost weight over the years and in the second season they made me the maroon outfit," she says. "How much cleavage I showed depended on which one I wore, since they were all cut differently and some were lower than others. Then we got that green dress — the one you wanted to straighten out the neckline on all the time. I wasn't crazy about the dress because you had to take the whole thing off to go to the bathroom. But the underwear was fabulous. I had to wear a corset like a merry widow and then we had what I like to call the industrial strength, Starfleet regulation brassiere and this has become the standard uniform for every woman on *Star Trek*. That's because the women see me as me and then they see me as Troi and they go `I want a bra like that' because it adds inches where there really are none. It is kind of depressing at the end of the day when you take it off."

Sixth season, Troi received a wardrobe promotion when Captain Jelico ordered her into regulation duds in "Chain of Command." "She gives him a dirty look and the producers watched the dailies and said, `Hey, she looks good in that' Why hasn't she been wearing that for the last six years and saved us a fortune in costumes?'"

Issue #5 $3.95

Epi-log Journal

Nov.-Dec. 1992

The Television Journal of Science Fiction, Fantasy, and Adventure

Gene Roddenberry Tribute Issue!
PART ONE: *Star Trek* * *Star Trek II* * *Star Trek: The Next Generation* * Genesis II * Planet Earth * Strange New World

....